MW01140467

*you ... of the Clyde*

# HIGH SCHOOL
# **Edubabble**

## A TEACHER-TALK GLOSSARY

## CLYDE WOOLMAN

 FriesenPress

Suite 300 - 990 Fort St
Victoria, BC, V8V 3K2
Canada

www.friesenpress.com

**Copyright © 2020 by Clyde Woolman**
First Edition — 2020

All rights reserved.

No part of this publication may be reproduced in any form, or by any means, electronic or mechanical, including photocopying, recording, or any information browsing, storage, or retrieval system, without permission in writing from FriesenPress.

ISBN
978-1-5255-6472-7 (Hardcover)
978-1-5255-6473-4 (Paperback)
978-1-5255-6474-1 (eBook)

*1. EDUCATION, REFERENCE*

Distributed to the trade by The Ingram Book Company

# BOOKS BY CLYDE WOOLMAN

## EDUCATION NOVELS

Dragons at the Schoolhouse Door: A Novel of Schooling – *FriesenPress 2020*

Hepting's Road: A Novel of Teaching – *FriesenPress 2018*

## EDUCATION SATIRE SERIES

High School Edubabble: A Teacher-Talk Glossary – *FriesenPress 2020*

Edubabble: A Glossary of Teacher Talk – *FriesenPress 2018*

## YOUNG ADULT ADVENTURE NOVELS – THE BEN TAVERS SERIES

Yurek: Edge of Extinction – *Moosehide Press 2013*

Smugglers at the Lighthouse – *Moosehide Press 2010*

For more information - www.clydewoolman.com

# ABOUT THE AUTHOR

Clyde Woolman has been a teacher, counselor, and principal of three high schools, a middle, and an elementary school. For six years he was a Superintendent of Schools (CEO) in a school district on Vancouver Island, British Columbia.

Having doled out his fair share of edubabble and after experiencing the governing bureaucracy first hand, he voluntarily returned to a school, finishing his career as a principal.

He has authored countless reports on school and district programs and chaired numerous committees tasked with reporting on school effectiveness.

He has always felt that those who worked directly in the classroom were subject to too much pontificating from those who either had never done the job or were far removed from it. This list of people included politicians, bureaucrats, school board members, and education professors and theorists.

Now retired, Clyde lives on Vancouver Island and divides his time between there, metropolitan Vancouver, and Maui.

TO ALL THE TEACHERS IN PUBLIC EDUCATION;

MAY YOU KEEP ON DOING THE GOOD THAT YOU DO,

AND KEEP YOUR SENSE OF HUMOR WHEN DOING IT.

# ACKNOWLEDGMENTS

Many thanks are extended to these educators for
stimulating my interest in Arts education:
Dave Brummitt, Nancy Cox, and Dale Hallier in Music,
Vicki Matthew and Lori Mazey in Theater,
Neil Crouch, Keith Rice-Jones, and Joe Stefiuk
in Visual Art;
Helene McGall, in all aspects of Arts education.

Appreciation is extended to the following teachers for
helping me develop a nascent understanding of Science
education; John Carswell and Roy Londry.

It is always challenging to read early drafts of manu-
scripts. Teachers John Carswell, Nancy Cox, Roy Londry,
and Brian Pitman provided valuable insight for much-
needed improvements.

As always, special appreciation is extended to my loving wife, life partner, and fellow teacher, Ileana Woolman.

# PREFACE

I have had the good fortune of being involved in education from a variety of vantage points—as a teacher, counselor, principal of five schools, as a central office bureaucrat, and a Superintendent (CEO). I have witnessed teachers, students, and administrators triumph over seemingly insurmountable challenges, having done so with noble spirit and good grace. On rare occasions I have seen a small cadre from each group display activity that defied logic or common sense.

High school teachers speak a common language, dotted with acronyms and jargon few in the profession probe for real meaning. Schools may be quite different across the United States and Canada, but the teachers who work in them share a common organizational culture created by the realities of their workplace. This shared culture and language is found in buildings large and small, in settings rural, suburban, and urban core. Though the specific terms and issues change, the essence of the shared culture and language continue, lending credence to the familiar saying, "The more things change, the more they stay the same."

Edubabble is a form of educator communication involving the use of ridiculously fluffy words and silly sloganeering. Since schools are likely to exist in the foreseeable future, the comedy of student shenanigans, the oft-times quirky teacher talk, and the proliferation of instructional jargon will continue. The seemingly unending batch of material prompted this sequel—*High School Edubabble,* to the earlier (2018) *Edubabble: A Glossary of Teacher Talk.* Aspects of edubabble can also be found in the comedic and somewhat zany new education novel, *Dragons at the Schoolhouse Door: A Novel of Schooling,* which follows the earlier (2018) *Hepting's Road: A Novel of Teaching.* Hollywood is not the only place where sequels are alive and well.

There are certain thematic threads that run through *High School Edubabble.* As with the first *Edubabble,* there are listings that focus on the school as a unique workplace, such as Bake Sale Comeback, Experiential Learning, Grad Hug, Plagiarism, Restroom Graffiti, and Time Vampires. The descriptions of the quirks and foibles of teacher, principal, and parent behavior, as well as the jargon associated with fads and trends in instructional practice, form a theme and a significant portion of the glossary.

It would be ridiculous for a satirical work such as this to not contain a thread pertaining to the impact of technology on teachers and students. Unlike previous generations, today's teachers face tech-addled youths who are drowning in a churning sea of information, much of it of dubious quality. Hopefully some humor can be found in descriptions such as Digital Citizenship, Fortnite, Screen

Addicts, Monks of the Digital Age, and Textbook (an interesting combination of texting and Facebook).

If one is seeking to inject some level of humanness into the technophilic teens of today, there may be no better choice than the Arts. This arts-orientation comprises the third broad thrust in the glossary—Acting, Art Supplies, Balanced Band, Improvisation, Jesus Christ Superstar, and Orchestral Class, is a small selection of Arts-oriented listings. Other entries, such as Mickey Mouse and New Art Form note the link between artistic creativity and technology.

The fourth theme includes entries related to the seeming decline of ethical standards in politics, business, and journalism. Schools do not operate in a vacuum. It is difficult for teachers to maintain a standard of expectation for youth to tell the truth, to listen to other viewpoints in a respectful manner, and to ensure that they have factual information before making decisions, when that behavior appears to be absent from many political leaders. There are many listings in *High School Edubabble* that make comment on this dichotomy between behavior expected and that witnessed. Anti-Educators, Ethical Standards, Journalism, Talking Heads, and Weapons of Mass Distortion are examples.

The fifth overarching theme is Science education. With an academic background in the Humanities, I knew very little about Science. Perhaps this lack of knowledge stimulated an interest in much the same way as my appreciation of the Arts developed over time. Unlike the Arts, which always seems to be battling a non-core image,

Science and related technology are currently hot-ticket items in many school jurisdictions. Perhaps that is why so many fields wish to be labeled a Science, as noted in the entries Learning Science, Management Science, Library Science, and Family and Consumer Science. These listings and others, such as Chemistry Teachers, Frog Dissections, Kilometer, and Uniqueness of Science Teachers, are but some of the other entries connected to Science education.

Finally, I must add a qualifying statement identical to the one listed in the preface of the first glossary. The themes are wrapped with intended humor. Of course, what constitutes humor depends upon the perception of the receiver, not the teller. As an educator, I am not a comedian. I do not tell jokes well as have never regarded myself as wryly sarcastic. I have tried to insert what I believe to be at least a dose of dry wit in most of the entries. There are comments offered for over three hundred terms or phrases. I hope people will find at least a few describe a truth hidden within the humor. I am sure some readers will groan at what they believe to be poor comedic satire expressed in some of the listings. Others may manage only a mild snicker at a comment or two. Some may be insulted by a few descriptions that "hit too close to home."

A teaching career is a wonderful yet challenging expedition that is full of adventure. Hopefully a little *High School Edubabble* humor can help navigate the more difficult terrain and make the journey that is teaching in high schools all the more enjoyable.

Good luck and good reading.

# A

**ABSTINENCE** There are a lot of tough "gigs" when you're teaching, such as being in front of an eleventh-grade "basic-level" Math group on a sunny Friday afternoon or a ninth-grade English class studying a Shakespearean sonnet. A tenth-grade history group studying the Renaissance on the final day before a major holiday can present a pedagogical hurdle for the most skilled teacher. These are but a few examples on a register of top instructional challenges. Teaching abstinence in a "sex-education" class to hormone-ravaged early teens certainly must be placed on such a list, likely in the top three. Good luck! *see also, David and Goliath, Gateway Drug, Ranking of Schools.*

**ACRONYMS** Why are acronyms so popular in education? One reason is the proficiency of some educator "theorists" to create edubabble. With the plethora of so much long-winded phraseology to explain relatively common-sensical approaches, sooner or later there is a need for abbreviations and acronyms to keep it all understandable. Like an educator's version of a catch-22, the acronym itself then becomes yet another example of edubabble; *see also, CHAP, Edubabble-Tangible (c).*

**ACTING** An excellent confidence-booster and form of self-expression for young people, this subject may not have realized its full potential. While it has been regarded as the focal point in drama and theater departments, there are alternate benefits. Skills that acting hones can be useful in politics and business. Politicians need to exude understanding even when they are clueless about an issue. They may be expected to ooze compassion when they really don't give a hoot, or emit *gravitas* when they would rather be in a bar enjoying a scotch and soda. Business CEO's have to evoke integrity when responding to evidence that the product they foisted on consumers is knowingly defective. Acting ability is a core skill for the powerful in the visual-oriented world of the 24/7 news cycle; *see also, Congress, Ethical Standards, Improvisation.*

**ACTION - ACTIVE** More than a few educational theorists and bureaucrats are fond of tacking on "action" or "active" as adjectives in front of just about any term they can find. There are action plans to be developed, active research to be undertaken, and active listening to be utilized. There is a need for teachers to be "active participants" in meetings, despite how boring or nonsensical the topic. Students should engage in "active" exercise (opposed, presumably to the inactive variety). They must be "actively engaged" in classroom activities (instead of napping or daydreaming). A principal has to be "action-oriented" (as opposed to lethargic). Adding the action or active adjective connotes drive, energy, and enthusiasm while augmenting the mystique of edubabble; *see also, Administrative Software Rollout, Edubabble-Characteristics (a)*.

**ACTION RESEARCH** This is great specific edubabble connected to the Action-Active entry above. It connotes drive and energy coupled with the intellectual pursuits involved in research. Yet it means little more than drivel. Doing research involves action. And it is nothing more than common sense to take at least some form of action as a result of that research when it is completed. After all, just as not deciding is a decision, ignoring the results of the research is a form of action; *see also, Action-Active, Edubabble-Characteristics (a)*.

**ADMINSTRATIVE SOFTWARE ROLLOUT** No one in an administrative position calls a new computer system, a "Management Software Program." The preferred term is "Administrative Software Rollout." The term "management" has a poor connotation in the relatively "soft" world of education. The term "rollout" provides a sense of planning coupled with action. Rollout really means that full implementation will take much longer than originally promised. The "techies" will try to blame the glitches (software only has glitches, not problems) on the tech-illiterate educators who fail to understand the beauty of the system that was created to supposedly make their paperwork chores easier; *see also, Action–Active.*

**ANTI-EDUCATORS** Teachers face significant challenges and the increasing number of anti-educators do not make the task any easier. What makes these people so insidious is their media presence and the wide range of positions they occupy in society. Some notable anti-educators are:

    a) President Trump who boasts that he does not read much; *see also, Congress, Digital Citizenship, Name-Calling;*

    b) The producers of TV shows such as *The Simpsons* which portray boys to be mindless dolts; *see also, Dumbing Down;*

    c) Celebrities such as the fluff-queen Kardashians who manage to become rich and famous without having accomplished anything;

    d) Athletes who exude an image of a spoiled brat by being solely interested in the truckloads of money they make;

    e) Members of Congress who, during an inquiry, clearly are more interested in scoring political points than seeking the truth; *see also, Congress, Hollow Promises–Students, Interrupting.*

**APPLES AND TREES** For the most part, the apple does not fall far from the tree. The respectful, polite student most often has respectful, polite parents. The rude obnoxious students have parents with similar tendencies. More than once in a teacher's career, frustration and annoyance will build about a particularly insolent student. There will be a meeting with the parents who are far more odious than the adolescent. Suddenly the teacher will see the student in a new light—the teen being remarkably well behaved given the parental role models and the genetic pool from which they derived; *see also, Bad Egg of the Family.*

**ARCHERY** It makes perfect sense to ban weapons from schools. But some schools actually hand weapons to students in PE class and then encourage their use. Arrows are used in archery. Anyone unlucky enough to have one pierce the flesh will attest that arrows are very effective weapons. More commonly seen in PE classes are spears, though to be fair the teachers call them javelins; *see also, Field Events, Knitting.*

**ASSISTANT PRINCIPAL** This title is a far better term than the old term, Vice-Principal. All one has to do is look up the meaning of vice to know why; *see also, Block Schedule, Naming of Positions.*

**ATTENTION ECONOMY** The economists have finally discovered what teachers have known for a long time— that attention is difficult to obtain and even harder to keep. Economists and marketers are beginning to regard attention as a scarce commodity in this consumptive age. With so much stimuli, how does one get and hold attention for any length of time? More importantly, hold it at least long enough that the business is able to sell something?

Teachers have struggled with this issue for some time. The challenge is more daunting now since the students have attention spans that resemble those of gnats. Teachers have little chance in any competition with the marketers. They are selling knowledge and skills, which are not nearly as sexy or exciting as a new video game or tech device. Compounding the challenge is that the tools teachers have at their disposal do not include sophisticated marketing data, internet tracking software, and up-to-the-minute hardware. Given the obstacles faced, teachers are remarkably skilled in grabbing what little student attention is available; *see also, Attention Deficit Disorder, David and Goliath, Lockers.*

**ATTENTION JUNKIES** These unfortunate souls are caught in the web of addiction. Once ensnared, it is difficult to extricate oneself. When they need a fix, they need one badly. Like their narcotic-famished brethren they will do anything to get what they need, including engaging in outlandish behavior or making the most asinine comments imaginable. In response, the teacher acts as the supplier, having to dole out more and more attention to keep the craving at bay. The needy adult is similar, as the forever-pontificating know-it-all colleague holds court in the teachers' lounge; *see also, Absenteeism-Student, Crisis Junkies, Know-It-All Colleague.*

**AUDITIONS** In an era of self-directed learning based on individual choice, how does a theater teacher select students for various roles? In fact, in the newly fashionable educational vibe, should the teacher be involved at all? And who chooses the play or musical to be performed? If it is the teacher, is that action not imposing external will on the students? How will that affect their self-esteem? Will they be interested in participating when they did not choose the play to be performed or the part they wish to have? Given these serious questions it is a wonder that schools were able to stage theatrical productions in the past and that all concerned actually enjoyed the experience; *see also, Balanced Band, Heutagogy.*

# B

**BAD EGG OF THE FAMILY** When a person has taught in the same school for a number of years there is a good possibility that siblings will eventually be enrolled. If the previous teen from that family has been intelligent, respectful, and polite there will be a natural tendency to expect the same from the sibling. This is true with many families. But not all. Beware that siblings can be diametric opposites. If the first of the brood was especially quiet, the bad egg is a rude blabbermouth. If the previous student was highly motivated, the bad egg is spectacularly slothful. No one knows what causes bad eggs to appear, though the desire to establish a separate identity from the sibling is a logical assumption; *see also, Apples and Trees.*

**BAKE SALE COMEBACK** The profit margins for old-fashioned cupcake sales are woefully inadequate to meet the extra needs of schools today. But with the legalization of pot (weed) in several US states and across Canada, opportunity arises. Weed-laced cupcakes could be sold to parents at concerts, theatrical productions, sports events, and graduations. The margins could be kept slim to keep the price tag low since the school could rely on sheer quantity of sales to generate impressive revenue; *see also, David and Goliath (5), Gateway Drug, Weed.*

**BALANCED BAND** Most students entering a high school beginner band want to play the sax, guitar, flute, or drums. Someone has to play the tuba or euphonium, and it is the teacher who has to make the decision. This teacher "intervention" flies in the face of the education world's move to self-directed, choice learning. A band is not made up solely of sax players but that's what it might look like if the teacher allowed students to determine how their personalized learning was to proceed. How band teachers manage to build a relatively balanced band in an era of student choice is a notable feat that goes largely unnoticed; *see also, Auditions, Euphonium, Heutagogy, Mason.*

**BASEBALL** It is surprising that this game is played in Physical Education classes when for ninety percent of the time only three players, pitcher, catcher, and to some extent the batter, are engaged in anything resembling physical activity. Aside from the student at the plate, the rest of the batting team is lolling about in the dugout, some paying attention, most not.

Aside from the pitcher and catcher, the only extra physical activity the members of the fielding team have over their dugout-shuttered opponents is that they are standing rather than sitting (the exception to this is the right fielder who may be lying on the grass). Standing on one's feet apparently works off more calories than sitting on one's buttocks. One benefit—after this "workout" there is no need to hit the showers; *see also, Jell-O, Losing Seasons (a).*

**BIOLOGY - REPTILES** On occasion a group of teachers may have a debate regarding the specific challenges facing those teaching high school as opposed to those instructing middle-school students. Rather than listing the various hurdles encountered at each level, a simple example can provide greater illumination.

Assuming for a minute that the teacher has brought a large caged snake into the classroom. The seventh-graders will cause near-pandemonium. They will be jostling for the best position from which to gawk at the reptile and fill the air with frenetic gushed statements such as, "Cool, a snake," or "Does it bite?" or "Gross, it's all scaly." When the same snake is brought into a senior Biology class, the students will stare at the creature with a modicum of interest before eventually asking, "Is this going to be on the test?"

**BLOCK SCHEDULE** It usually only takes high school students a week before they understand the complexities and nuances of their school's method of scheduling classes (for some teachers it takes a little longer). What appears complicated soon becomes the mundane.

The following is a suggestion for any high school principal with a warped sense of humor who wishes to cause chaos throughout the school among teachers and students alike. Firstly, the entire episode must be kept secret from the Assistant Principal(s). Before the first class is to begin, sidle over to the microphone for the public address system. After gurgling into the mike to clear the phlegm from the throat, announce something akin to, "Today, instead of day three it will be day one of your schedule. Block C will be first period instead of block A. Block D will occur tomorrow instead of this afternoon."

This should be repeated once more, with a moderate level and tone of voice. You will feel the vibes throughout the school as students and faculty members stop and ask each other, "What was that? What did he say?" Those people that caught more of the announcement might wonder aloud, "Why is it day one today? It's supposed to be day three." For the best impact, and for personal safety, head to your car with the engine running for the quickest getaway possible. Smile as you drive away knowing your various assistants are attempting to control the resultant mayhem; *see also, Assistant Principal.*

**BOARDING SCHOOL SYNDROME** British psychologist Joy Schaverien coined this term and wrote a notable book about it in 2015. She never attended a boarding school but discovered that a disproportionate number of her patients had. Separated from families, frequently bullied and traumatized, she found that many of these privileged youth suffered from psychological distress in adulthood.

Perhaps unfairly, those that suffered such trauma are not likely to receive a great deal of sympathy. After all, the family made the boarding school choice (though the youth likely had very little say in the matter). Unlike the church-run residential schools in North America, the intent of the British boarding schools was to perpetuate the culture of the privileged in an impressive setting, not eliminate a language and culture in barely adequate facilities. However, if Schaverien is correct, there may be some psychological similarities between those sent off to perpetuate the elite and those forced to attend institutions designed to obliterate a culture.

**BODY SHAMING** Though it is obvious when a person's shape does not fit within the broad parameters of normal, it is best that a teacher not only refrain from any comments but reprimand students who do so. Commenting that a student is tall, short, hefty, or slender can result in accusations of body shaming, even when the comment is made in a positive light. Unless students are mentally or visually handicapped, by the ninth grade they have a pretty good idea of what their body looks like when compared to others. If they don't, that is an issue in itself; *see also, Frog Dissections.*

**BOOKWORM** Before the age of computers (and for young teachers there really was such an era), students who were self-absorbed with reading were often labeled bookworms. This was generally a derogatory term and the youngsters in question were often social isolates. If they continued with their love of books and relative lack of social contact there were only a few occupations that matched their interest—museum curator, librarian, archivist to name a few. None of these professions was particularly lucrative.

In today's world, those with bookwormish tendencies have shifted from printed material to computers, especially video games. Being adept at these activities can lead to a financial windfall in competitions. A person can also branch into computer hacking, where there are considerably less-than-legal opportunities to make a boat-load of money spying for corporations or foreign governments such as Russia; *see also, Endangered Species-Students, Fortnite, Jell-O, Screen Addicts, World Cup of Gaming.*

**BOWLING TEAM** One of the main deterrents to a student joining this team is not that the "sport" is uncool. Aside from the big three of football, baseball, and basketball, sports can become in-vogue and just as quickly return to uncool status with notoriously unpredictable teens. What may be the real deterrent for bowling is the fashion statement that is made by wearing a decidedly uncool shirt made of spongy polyester. The get-up may appear retro but still looks dorky. A teacher wishing to spice up the image and recruit new team members may wish to start with a new-look bowling shirt.

**BRAIN-BASED LEARNING** This phrase is excellent edubabble since it is impressive sounding while actually making no sense. It is difficult to imagine any learning that does not emanate from brain activity; *see also, Edubabble-Characteristics (c)*.

**BREVITY IS THE SOUL OF WIT** If this familiar saying has validity, then many politicians and news network panelists must join edubabblers and education professors in the witless category; *see also, Congress, Interrupting*.

# C

**CANNED PRESENTATIONS** Conferences featuring corporate-based professional development is now the order of the day. In many ways these resemble a corporate pitch. The speaker promotes a new program complete with books, CD's, and software packages available for sale in the lobby after the talk. Nothing is left to chance. The music is canned. The technology is canned. The script is canned. Even the jokes are canned (and corny). Chances are a teacher will have forked out a fair amount of money to hear the sales pitch; *see also, Conferences, Edupreneurs.*

**CAPSTONE LEARNING** Educators are not shy about borrowing terminology from other occupations. This entry is a good example. A capstone is the final stone placed on top of a wall or monument. A capstone project is the culminating student project, most often at the conclusion of high school. Because this term makes sense, it does not meet the definition of edubabble; *see also, Concept Maps, Edubabble.*

**CAREER EDUCATION** *see Job Shadowing.*

**CATASTROPHIZING** Is it any wonder that anxiety and depression are on the rise among the young when at least some teachers spend a good portion of classroom time basically expounding that the world is, "Going to hell in a handbasket?" While it is essential to discuss climate change, habitat reduction, jihadism, racism, environmental degradation and the like, it is also important to make note of the positive changes over the last fifty years. There are many—the rise in the standard of living in many previously impoverished countries, the increasing acceptance of women in leadership roles, the growing popularity of electric cars, and the connectivity that technology provides, to name a few major thrusts. While it is true that each one of these issues creates challenges, a little balance in presentation would go a long way to helping youth find positive solutions to the challenges rather than wallowing in helplessness and apathy; *see also, Xanax.*

**CHAP** An acronym for a modern and enlightened method for dealing with student misbehavior—Cajole, Humor, and Plead; *see also, Acronyms.*

**CHEMISTRY TEACHERS** Chemists have been regarded as pseudo-magicians (15th century alchemists), heroic science pioneers (19th century Currie, Nobel, and Pasteur), and mad scientists (20th Century horror movies). In contemporary times there are a number of quick-to-judge activists who regard some Chemistry majors to be happily assisting nefarious corporations. By experimenting with all manner of ill-advised chemicals being placed into food, water, and even clothing, these scientists are regarded as more focused on their own and corporate bottom line than in benefitting humanity.

The activists may have a dilemma of conscience if they ever set their sights on those people with Chemistry degrees who chose a career teaching in high schools. The teachers do not engage in ethically dubious experimentation nor are they consumed with corporate profit. Their personal bottom line, as reflected in their meager teacher paycheck, would most often be a fraction of that of the "corporate chemist."

As often the case with those that rail against the science of today, broad generalizations rarely reflect the entire story; *see also, Farnsworth, Teacher Shortage-Math and Science, Uniqueness of Science Teachers (2).*

**COLLABORATION** Somewhere, sometime, a teacher has had to listen to a line such as, "Our school's collegial culture leads to collaboration, culminating in collective consensus." The statement is a good example of edubabble bordering on gibberish; it is also excellent alliteration; *see also, Edubabble, Gibberish.*

**CONCEPT MAPS** These are graphic organizers used by students to connect ideas, concepts, and terms. The salient issue is to break down the central concept into component parts. Unlike most edubabble, the term is a relatively accurate description of the activity; *see also, Flowcharts.*

**CONFERENCES** Conferences are for every educator, or so many brochures claim. The ASCD 2018 Boston Empower18 Conference had a regular registration fee just shy of $700.00 for non-members ($600.00 for members). If travel, meals, and lodging are included that could easily reach a $1,500.00 tab which might stretch most teachers' professional development allocation.

At least conference organizers welcome any teacher who can afford to attend. This is not so with summits and symposiums. According to one event marketing agency, summits differ from conferences in that they are intended for "high level" professionals. Symposiums are even more elite since they are described as events where "experts" give presentations; *see also, Canned Presentations, Swag.*

**CONFLICT OF INTEREST** Teachers are usually aware of, and avoid, conflicts of interest, such as receiving money for tutoring a student in their class, or having their spouse act as their substitute teacher when sick. This may not always be the case in some universities where professors conduct "impartial" research while receiving a grant from a corporation and assigning their own (or their friend's) textbook as required reading for their course; *see also, Edupreneurs.*

**CONGRESS** It is extremely difficult for a teacher to insist on decorum in class while students discuss controversial topics when the behavior of men and women in Congress, and those working in the White House, border on impolite at best and rude at worst; *see also, Acting, Anti Educators (a) (e), Brevity is the Soul of Wit, Ethical Standards, Interrupting, Journalism, Weapons of Mass Distortion.*

**CRISIS JUNKIES** There is nothing better than a perceived crisis to get the blood flowing to start or end the day. And for the few teachers who are afflicted with this malady, schools provide plenty of opportunity to find a crisis around every corner. There are only eight paint brushes in the Art storeroom when there should be ten! The students were talking in the assembly! Five students were in the hallway without a pass! There is no white paper in the photocopy room! Somebody's car is in my parking stall! Why isn't anyone doing anything to solve these critical issues?

However, as with all junkies, providing a fix only provides temporary relief to the yearning. Colleagues know that as soon as one issue is resolved for the crisis junkie, another will appear soon thereafter—and another, and another, and another after that; *see also, Attention Junkies, Kleenex Box, Know-it-All Colleague.*

**CULINARY CORRECTNESS** Vending machines are being hauled out of many high schools. Where can a young person in a school get a twinkie, soda, or bag of chips these days? *see also, Kale, Quinoa, Vending Machines.*

**CURRICULUM - PROCESS / PRODUCT** There are learned people who actually care about the distinction between curriculum as process or as product. They write articles about it using ten-dollar words when a one-dollar bill would do. They are not likely teachers who are too busy working with students. As a mercifully brief note, curriculum as a process regards curriculum as the interaction of teachers, students, and knowledge. The curriculum-as-a-product advocates regard education as a technical enterprise with objectives set and outcomes measured. Given the increasingly corporate and managerial tinge to education, the curriculum as product view definitely has the upper hand; *see also, Canned Presentations, Quibble (5).*

# D

**DALI, SALVADOR** *see Expulsion from School (1),*
*Website Project.*

**DAVID AND GOLIATH** Teachers are well aware of the
tale of David and Goliath as a metaphor that has tran-
scended its religious roots. Many teachers face similar
odds every day, taking on a formidable adversary and
coming out on top more often than one would think.
Examples are:
1. Theater teachers demonstrating how the world of
   the stage can have as much, or more, emotional
   impact on youth than that derived from yet
   another Marvel special-effects blockbuster; *see
   also, Acting.*
2. Art teachers showing that absorbing visuals were
   produced by talented humans before computers
   were invented; *see also, Website Design Project.*
3. Foods teachers trying to teach nutrition while
   battling ads for sugary pop, occasionally promoted

by their own school; *see also, Vending Machines.*

4. Algebra teachers explaining why the subject is relevant.

5. History teachers trying to convince students that studying the past helps a person understand the present.

6. Counselors organizing anti-drug and alcohol groups while pot is legalized in an increasing number of jurisdictions and teens are convinced that virtually every adult is on some form of medication; *see also, Abstinence, Bake Sale Comeback, Gateway Drug, Juul.*

7. All teachers attempting to teach the proper use of English in an era of tech-driven verbiage; *see also, Unfriend.*

**DEADLINE** Most teachers have worked with at least one curmudgeonly colleague who often complains about students being late when completing assignments. Often it is this teacher who exceeds the deadline in submitting report cards or other information to the office. "I'm too busy to adhere to those timelines," is a frequent explanation, failing to miss the irony before launching another broadside about student lethargy; *see also, Kleenex Box, Meeting Behavior-Teachers (e), Toxicity Pit.*

**DIGITAL CITIZENSHIP** Teachers and other responsible adults encourage youth to make good use of the internet. Unfortunately, some adults in powerful positions are forever tweeting up a storm and the tone used would not pass the digital citizenship bar set for third-graders; *see also, Anti-Educators (a), Ethical Standards, Manners-Teaching of, Weapons of Mass Distortion.*

**DIMINUTIVE NICKNAMES - BOYS** At what age should a teacher cease to use the diminutive nickname for boys? Such names are rarely applied to teens or adults except in male locker rooms. Referring to Bill, Tim, and Lamar and as Billy, Timmy, and Lammy outside the confines of locker-room banter does not seem to be appropriate for beefy teenage boys.

**DINKY DISTRICTS** School districts in the United States range in size from New York City with just over one million students, to those with one tiny K-9 or K-12 school. Small-sized districts provide excellent examples of needless bureaucracy. Just what does a Superintendent of Schools do all day when the district has one or two miniscule schools—nap, read education journals, watch *Judge Judy* on TV? With so little to do, the superintendent may spend time getting in the way of the principal who also has problems searching for an activity to help fill in a long day. The superintendent is the Chief Officer of the School Board so having coffee with trustees is at least a passable activity; *see also, Gargantuan Districts, Parkinson's Law.*

**DISAGGREGATED DATA** What a potentially fine edubabble phrase! There's a ten-dollar word (disaggregated), a five-dollar word (data), and even a little bit of alliteration thrown in. However, a reasonably educated person can deduce that this term essentially means to break data down into specific groups, such as Indigenous students or those of African-American ancestry. Since one key purpose of edubabble is to obfuscate, this term falls a bit short; *see also, Edubabble-Characteristics (c)*.

**DISCIPLINE - STUDENTS** Parents who want firm discipline in the schools usually intend it for the other kids, not their own.

**DISTRIBUTED LEADERSHIP** This is good edubabble since it appears to link with flat hierarchies and teacher empowerment. The positive interpretation of this activity is that the leader is confident and trusting enough to leave the work in the hands of others by constantly delegating. Of course, there is another interpretation. The leader may be incompetent, lazy, or both; *see also, Flat Hierarchies*.

**DOCTORATE DEGREES IN EDUCATION** Education is one of the few disciplines (if it really meets that standard) in which there are two separate doctoral degrees, the EdD and the PhD. The EdD is intended for those practicing educators who wish to conduct research in schools by examining the impact of new programs and methodology. Such research activity raises more than a few questions about using students as "guinea pigs" but that is for comment in another entry; *see also, Guinea Pig Students*.

The PhD program is generally intended for those who want to work in academia, conduct research, and ... well ... work in academia and conduct more research; *see also, Journal of Learning Sciences, Neuroscience, Oligarchs in Education (a) (d).*

**DRACULA** *see Varney the Vampire, Young Adult Gothic Horror.*

**DRESS CODE - TEACHERS** It may be difficult for principals to implement "professional" dress codes for teachers in today's world when some jeans for women can cost more than a dress, and men's designer polo shirts can be more costly than dress shirts. There is a line however, though it is rarely codified. Portions of outfits that may cause at least some controversy are:

    a) A T-shirt with, "Beer; it's not just for breakfast anymore," emblazoned across the front;

    b) Five-inch stiletto heels adorning a woman's, or man's, feet;

    c) A black balaclava;

    d) Underwear as outerwear.

**DRONES** These machines are good for more than dropping bombs on distant villages. They can deliver medical supplies to isolated areas and provide aerial photography for mapping and exploration. They could also be excellent supervision tools for schools to more effectively monitor school property. Drones are cheaper than supervision aides, don't complain about anything, and, if teachers are doing the supervision, can release them from a task most regard as tedious.

Initially, a few students may fire projectiles at the drones, but they'll soon tire of that activity. If the supervising drone is kept at a high enough altitude, most of the kid's throws will miss anyway.

This would not be the first time that educators have "borrowed" ideas from the military; *see also, Crisis Junkies, Hallway Monitors, Intelligence Testing–Masses.*

**DRONING** If teachers and students were more involved in selecting principals, they may choose more activity-oriented tests rather than the traditional interview. One such scenario may be to ascertain how the candidate intervenes to prevent a physical alteration. Another may be reading a notice over the school's public address (PA) system. If the candidate drones on and on it can lull everyone into a zone resembling sleep or mindless texting. This defeats the purpose of the PA system, which is to transmit information to an audience that is at least minimally awake and/or aware. A low mark on the PA scenario might cause insufferably monotone principal candidates to be unsuccessful in obtaining the leadership position; *see also, Public Address System, Zoned Out.*

**DROP OUT RATE** The public expects a great deal from the education system. Politicians want even more. They want "standards" especially if there is any inkling that the public feels these are slipping. Then the politicians start teacher-roasting. But the politicians also want high graduation rates, especially if they feel the public thinks there are too many teens not attending school.

It is easy to develop a system where everyone will graduate—simply lower the standards to such a point that any barely-attending sloth-like student can receive a diploma. It is also easy for the system to raise standards. But if the bar is set too high, many students will not be able to reach it.

The system has done well balancing these factors despite what some politicians say. Standards have remained relatively stable and the drop-out rate in the United States has declined from 27% in 1960 to 12% in 1990. By 2010 the drop out rate was even lower, at just over 7% (6.3% for females and 8.5% for males); *see also, Special Education, Under the Bus.*

**DUMBING DOWN** It is decidedly uncool for a boy to appear intelligent while traversing the treacherous journey through the early to mid-teen years. Dumbing down is a good way to establish social acceptability among the macho wannabe peers and thus contribute to emotional (and physical) safety; *see also, Anti-Educators (b).*

# E

**EARLY PUBLIC EDUCATION** It is difficult to fathom that in its infancy some people believed that public education was a ridiculously expensive social experiment bound to go wrong. Though concessions were made by the system (such as summer months away from school so youth could work on the farm), public education was regarded by some as unnecessary. After all, it was argued that not everyone needed to learn to read and write. And educating every citizen could lead to dangerous levels of knowledge among the "masses." These types of arguments had much in common with the response to other "crazy" ideas such as women attempting to achieve the right to vote or African-Americans and their supporters lobbying for basic civil rights; *see also, Year-Round Schools.*

**EAVESDROPPING** *see Grapevine-Student.*

**ECONOMIES OF SCALE** If economies of scale work in education as they allegedly do in business, high schools of 5,000 students and elementary schools of 1,000 or more would result in a much cheaper cost "per unit," in this case, the student. Additional benefits could accrue. Imagine the potential success for varsity sports teams when a coach has 5,000 students to choose from; *see also, Losing Seasons.*

**EDUBABBLE - CHARACTERISTICS** The following are some ways in which a person can identify solid edubabble:
   a) The word "action" or "active" is used as an adjective; *see also, Action-Active;*
   b) There is at least one word with three or more syllables;
   c) The word or phrase exudes complexity intended to obfuscate, though the actual meaning is simple or common-sensical; *see also, Brain-Based Learning, Disaggregated Data, Oracy;*
   d) A long and seemingly complex adjective is inserted prior to a simple noun; *see also Disaggregated Data, Heuristic Learning;*
   e) Any adjective that precedes the word, learning; *see also, Experiential Learning, Heuristic Learning, Situated Learning, Visual Learning;*

**EDUBABBLE - TANGIBLE** By definition edubabble can be difficult to decipher. If the entry above does not clarify matters, it may be beneficial to provide a few tangible analogies to use as examples:

    a) Edubabble as fluff—akin to dandruff falling on your shoulder. It is brushed away but keeps coming back;

    b) Edubabble as disconcerting jargon—like pollen in the spring, making some people feel uncomfortable;

    c) Edubabble as inhibiting understanding—comparable to a road filled with potholes that makes it difficult to reach a destination.

**EDUCATION MALPRACTICE** What if a teenager cannot read, write, add, or subtract? What if a youth has poor self-esteem due to bullying? What if a student has a victim persona due to the teacher's belittling? Perhaps an educational malpractice suit may be in order.

Setting a universal standard for duty of care, coupled with difficulties proving direct causation, have been particularly thorny issues for any litigants in education malpractice lawsuits. But that won't stop some teacher-bashing lawyers from giving it, "the old college try." For less-than-stellar tort law specialists, educational malpractice has a less sleazy ring, is easier, and safer, than chasing ambulances when trying to sign up a client and make a buck.

Heaven help teachers if these lawsuits begin to become successful in the future.

**EDUCATIONAL KINESIOLOGY** This term is quite a mouthful so Edu-K became the abbreviation and Brain

Gym became the more-catchy marketing title for the company that markets Edu-K paraphernalia. The proponents believe that the brain will develop, and learning will be enhanced, by specific body movements. Brain Gym is owned by the Educational Kinesiology Foundation, a non-profit based in where else—California?

**EDUPRENEURS** There have always been entrepreneurs working in conjunction with the education system. Often former teachers, they would sell all manner of material, supplies, and textbooks to school districts.

Now there is the edupreneur. This person works within the system and has an income-generating business linked to education, "on the side." They create courses and offer professional development sessions. They develop software and design supporting resource material. So, who owns material, the school district or the individual teacher? Does it matter if the material was developed in the school? Is it important that the district provides time for the teacher to give the training sessions? If the profits are to be shared, who gets the bigger slice of the pie?

If the pies begin to get large enough (and there is a good chance they will), expect a batch of lawyers to be gathering around with pie-slicing knives in hand; *see also, Canned Presentations, Conflict of Interest, Formula 1 Race Car Drivers, NewSchools Venture Fund.*

**ENDANGERED SPECIES - STUDENTS** *see Bookworm, Grease Monkeys.*

**ENDANGERED SPECIES - TEACHERS** As with many examples in the animal kingdom, there are endangered species within the teaching ranks. Some examples are:

a) male teachers wearing ties; *see also, Dress Code-Teachers, Image-Professorial;*

b) expectant female teachers wearing maternity dresses, preferring to follow the tight-clothing trend set by pregnant style-setting celebrities;

c) teachers who write notes on a board using chalk;

d) teachers who believe the principal is the "master" as per the tradition in English schools.

**ETHICAL STANDARDS** When the space satellite Sputnik was launched by the-then Soviet Union in 1957, there was a feeling that Americans were falling behind in Science and Technology. Money flowed like water in order to upgrade a perceived weakness. In the 1970s, when there was a belief that the state was not doing enough to promote racial integration, funds were plowed into school bussing. When there was a reform movement advocating change for public schools in the 1990's, legislation was altered and funds became available for Charter schools. When there was a perceived need to develop computer literacy post 2000, hardware and software was purchased by the truckload.

Whenever there has been a need to respond to a societal challenge or crisis, schools often receive support to initiate new programs.

Given the low level of ethical standards displayed by an increasing number of political and business leaders, perhaps schools will receive funds to meet the challenge of the ethical crisis; *see also, Acting, Anti-Educators, Congress, Digital Citizenship, Javert and Valjean, Journalism, Manners-Teaching Of, Popcorn, Smoke Pit, University Admission, Weapons of Mass Distortion.*

**EUPHONIUM** Any teacher of a beginner-band class may have a difficult time convincing a student to play the tuba, it being a rather large cumbersome instrument with an unhip name. However, a clever question such as, "How about playing the euphonium?" may elicit a positive response. The student will not know that the instrument is also large (though smaller than a tuba) and will likely be more favorable to the cool-sounding name; *see also, Balanced Band.*

**EVIDENCE-BASED PRACTICE** Education is not shy about borrowing terminology and practice from other fields, especially when such verbiage can contribute to edubabble. The concept of evidence-based practice originated from health care in the 1990s. Dr. David Sackett's 1996 definition is the most common. In part, he states that the term means, "Integrating individual expertise with the best available external clinical evidence from systematic research."

Whatever this really meant for those researching educational practice is a moot point. Anything that sounds that impressive is too good to pass up; *see also, Neuroscience.*

**EVOLUTION - TEACHING OF** *see Scopes, John.*

**EXPERIENTIAL LEARNING** This is a solid edubabble term since it is officious sounding with sub-categories that use ten-dollar words. Developed in the 1980s by David Kolb, there are four stages to Experiential Learning. For the purpose of this glossary, the proverbial child touching the hot stove will be the example.

a) Step 1—Official term, "Concrete Experience." Translated, this involves the child touching the hot element;

b) Step 2—Official term, "Reflective Observation." Translated, this has the child reflecting on the pain and shaking a hot hand to cool it off;

c) Step 3—Official term, "Abstract Conceptualization." Translated, this has the child concluding to not repeat such action unless he or she enjoys pain;

d) Step 4—Official term, "Active Experimentation." Translated, this means using what has been learned since in the future the child first holds the hand away from heat to gauge the temperature.

A parent does not have to have an education or psychology degree to understand "experiential learning." For that matter, neither does a child; *see also, Edubabble-Characteristics (e), Situated Learning, Visual Learning.*

**EXPULSION FROM SCHOOL** Teachers may believe that a student being expelled from school is a serious event. For the most part, that is true. However, the expelled or suspended student is in some pretty good company:

1. Salvador Dali was suspended from a Fine Arts Academy after one year for leading a student

protest in 1923. He returned to school only to be expelled again in 1926 for stating that his professors were not competent enough to help him; *see also, Website Project.*

2. Romantic poet Shelley was expelled from Oxford in 1811 for writing about the necessity of atheism; *see also, Romantic Poets (a).*

3. Edgar Allan Poe was kicked out of military school in 1831 for drinking and truancy.

4. William Randolph Hearst of journalism fame (and the man who allegedly was the inspiration for the movie *Citizen Kane*), was expelled from Harvard in 1885 for sending chamber pots to professors complete with their names and photos.

5. Marlon Brando was expelled in 1943 from two schools for truancy and general rabble rousing, including an apparent motorcycle ride through one high school (the movie *The Wild One* was released ten years later).

6. Eric "slow hand" Clapton of rock-guitar fame was suspended for constantly playing the instrument when at school.

# F

**FACSE** An abbreviation for Family and Consumer Sciences Education, this relatively newly-named department in many high schools presumably replaces the outdated title, Home Economics. In an age where science and technology are a dominant force in the culture and economy, every field of study wants to tack the word science onto the title. This is true even if the discipline has little to do with the scientific method and is about as far removed from traditional sciences as one can get; *see also, Learning Commons, Journal of Learning Sciences, Library Science, Names and Titles–Science.*

**FAKE NEWS** *see Anti–Educators (a), Ethical Standards, Journalism, Smoke Pit, Under the Bus, Weapons of Mass Distortion.*

**FARNSWORTH, PHILIO** Sometimes a teacher is behind a revolutionary idea. In 1920, fourteen-year-old Philio Farnsworth talked to his Chemistry teacher about an idea for an electronic imaging device. It was so complex he had to draw a diagram on the board and the teacher had to study it at length before commenting. The teacher applauded the idea and Philio kept working on it. Seven years later, Philio created a device which is generally recognized as being the main impetus behind the television; *see also, Chemistry Teachers.*

**F-BOMB** High school students barely notice when they use the 'F' word. It is used so often it resembles white noise. Teens will even debate whether the word should be categorized as profane or obscene. How can such a versatile word, excellent as an adverb, verb, adjective, or noun, be rude? *see also, Limerick, Manners-Teaching Of, Nantucket, Obscenity and Profanity, Oracy, White Noise (d).*

**FICTION AND REALITY** It does not take many years before a teacher realizes that escapades and episodes that once sounded like ridiculous fiction were actually real events in a school. Some of these may include:

a) a tenth-grade student with his or her head caught in a drainpipe;

b) students having an after-school sexual romp in an empty library;

c) a beefy male student bragging that he can eat twelve hamburgers in the school cafeteria—and then doing so before the inevitable stomach reaction occurs and sends him hurrying to a nearby toilet;

d) a student stocking an empty locker with soda-pop and undercutting the school's vending machines;

e) a ninth-grade student with his/her tongue stuck to a frozen flag pole.

The demarcation lines between fiction and reality in a school can certainly become blurred; *see also, Weapons of Mass Distortion.*

**FIELD EVENTS** There is little chance of serious injury in Track events beyond strained muscles and an ankle or two that suffered an unfortunate encounter with a hurdle. But field events are an entirely different matter. Injury lurks at any pit or throwing area. Students are given spears to fling, called javelins. At other times they get to use a pole to launch themselves high in the air and clear a bar. They are encouraged to hold a heavy iron ball and "put" it airborne, hopefully landing it with a thud in the sand rather than on a fellow student's toe. Hurling a heavy disk into the air seems easy. But not when it is done after the student twirls around a few times. The disorientation can cause a wild array of discus throws into unspecified areas, especially for the beginner. Given the popularity of these events in PE programs it is a wonder that there is not a steady parade of injured students heading to the medical room for much-needed repairs; *see also, Archery, Knitting.*

**FINE ARTS TEACHERS - SUPERIVISION OF** Opposites attract. This may be true in magnetism, electricity, and perhaps in romance. But bureaucrats and creative artists, virtual opposites in what they value, are not always a good match. This is especially evident in education when an unfortunate systems-oriented administrator is assigned to organize and supervise the Fine Arts teachers. Good luck to the teachers. Good luck to the administrator.

**FIRST-DAY FASHION** The texting will be furious and the phone lines buzzing the day before high school students will be returning to school. For many students, the fashion statement chosen for the first day places an indelible stamp on one's image. Social status is achieved if the reaction of others is positive. Bleak notoriety can follow if a fashion blunder is made and the resultant reaction is negative.

Fortunately, adults have grown past such shallowness, haven't they? *see also, Thumb Tapping.*

**FLAT HIERARCHIES** This now-popular notion is a good example of an edubabble technique; take a term such as hierarchy, and then add a descriptor to give a totally opposite meaning. Hierarchies represent a leveling of authority. They are, by definition, not flat.

Education organizations tend to downplay the traditional triangular hierarchy, preferring terms such as broad consensus, teacher empowerment, or shared leadership. While there is a great deal of edubabble about the positive aspects of such "flat" hierarchies, the variance in salary levels and the intensity of blame foisted on individuals when something goes awry, seems to indicate that not everything is as "shared" as one might be led to believe; *see also, Distributed Leadership.*

**FLOWCHARTS** A combination of webbing blended with a concept map, there must be reasons why administrators favor these graphic organizers. Usually designed to track information flow or decision-making processes, perhaps they are seen to bring systems-based order to unbridled chaos. Any teacher who has tried to follow the jumble of administrator-designed boxes, circles, and arrows on a too-small piece of paper would likely disagree; *see also, Concept Maps.*

**FORMULA 1 RACE CAR DRIVERS** These men, and some women, are walking billboards. So plastered is their garb with corporate logos they are best described as advertisements in human form. Perhaps teachers should jump on this bandwagon. Emulating these race-car drivers, they could wear jumpsuits with logos for software companies, copy machines, computers, and furniture. Specialty-area teachers could make extra money. PE teachers could advertise sports equipment and Music teachers instrument companies. Science teachers could get in on the action and wear logos of chemical suppliers. The only teachers presumably left out of this specialist bonanza would be the Math teachers with little else to hock except geometry sets and textbooks, both of which are rapidly moving out of vogue; *see also, Edupreneurs, Textbook.*

**FORTNITE** Unfortunately, too many young people are addicted to narcotics or alcohol. To make matters worse, there is a new "fix" available—video games. Fortnite is particularly addictive and a player has to use V-bucks to get more out of the "free" game. According to USA Today, in 2019 Fortnite had over 200 million users and there are competitions with prize money totalling in the millions of dollars. And teachers wonder why their students aren't doing school-issued homework; *see also, Gateway Drug, Jell-O, Screen Addicts, V-Bucks, World Cup of Fortnite, Zoned Out.*

**FREUDIAN SLIP** *see Ostracized, Phallic Symbol.*

**FROG DISSECTIONS** The most common animal used in science dissections is the frog. And while the practice is becoming more controversial, the activity remains a staple in most biology classrooms. But why the frog? Science teachers will explain that the organs in a frog and the way they are laid out are similar enough to humans to provide insight into how the human body functions. That in itself is a bit worrisome to laypeople who likely never considered their innards akin to that of a little reptile.

There are practical reasons as well. The frog is abundant and relatively small. Animals such as sea lions are difficult to catch and there is limited storage space for thirty of these or like-sized animals. The frog also has a short life span, so perhaps the rationale is something akin to, "What the hell, they're going to die soon anyway."

To be totally unscientific and at the risk of body-shaming the poor creature, frogs are not that appealing. If they were cute and fuzzy, they would have a far better chance of escaping the thrusts and cuts of scalpel-wielding students. That role would fall to some other unfortunate creature not blessed with a cuddly body and good looks; *see also, Body Shaming*.

**FRONT-OF-HOUSE** What is a director of a major school production to do when the decidedly pro-jock principal wants to volunteer to help? Front-of-house is a perfect role. The title sounds important so the principal will be happy. The role involves not much more than organizing the ushers, so the principal will be pleased about that too. In addition, greeting the crowds as they enter is a natural for any community relations-oriented leader, and who among them doesn't like to chat up parents and civic leaders?

# G

**GAME DESIGN** *see Bookworm, Fortnite, Mickey Mouse, New Art Form, V-Bucks, World Cup of Fortnite.*

**G AND T** Outside of education, G and T refers to Gin and Tonic, an especially popular drink during warm summer days. In education it usually refers to a Gifted and Talented program.

If a teacher in this program listens to enough edubabble about the differences between gifted and talented students, or a gifted as opposed to an enrichment program, it will likely lead the poor instructor to quaff more than a few tumblers of the real G&T, whether it be warm outside or not; *see also, Quibble (3), New Texting Abbreviations (d), Teacher of the Gifted.*

**GARGANTUAN DISTRICTS** There are approximately ten large metropolitan school districts in the United States under control of the mayor rather than a School Board. One of these is New York. The annual budget is close to twenty-five billion dollars (that is not a typo), and there are 1,800 separate schools (that is not a typo either). The flowchart for decision-making would likely take up a wall in a gymnasium.

With 75,000 teachers, the association would have to book Yankee Stadium on two successive days for a union meeting since that venue's capacity is only 54,251. All three auditoriums of Carnegie Hall would be needed for a meeting of the approximately 3,500 school-based administrators. If the Chancellor (Superintendent) spoke at those gatherings there would be more than a few in the audience who would not have a clue who the person was; *see also, Dinky Districts.*

**GATEWAY DRUG** It is much more difficult to sell the notion to students that marijuana is a gateway drug to a world of more powerful narcotics and a life of addiction-fueled misery when it is legal in many states and across the entire country in Canada; *see also, Abstinence, Bake Sale Comeback, David and Goliath (5), Zoned Out.*

**GENDERQUEER** It is not unusual for schools to feel the impact of significant social change. In a sense, schools can become staging areas and testing grounds for societal shifts. This occurred in the past during the civil rights and feminist movement. Today's seismic shift may be in the area of gender and has the potential to make the old controversies of teaching "sex education" look like a stroll in the park in comparison. Genderqueer is a contemporary catch-all phrase for those with gender identities that are not exclusively male or female (those who are flexible in their commitment to a single gender are gender fluid). There are those who are agender, bigender, trigender, and/or transgender.

This complexity is daunting, especially when civil rights lawyers are hovering about making sure the educator charged with teaching this new, complex material does not slip up. Many teachers will pine for the "old days" when sex education was a boring hash of basic biology terminology that stayed constant, at least for a few years; *see also, Joan of Arc, Leading Roles, Women's Suffrage.*

**GENERATION Z** First there were teachers from Generation X, then Gen Y, and now Generation Z. The moniker for the next generation will have to start at the beginning of the alphabet; *see also, iGen.*

**GIBBERISH** There may be confusion about the distinction between gibberish and edubabble. Merriam-Webster defines the noun gibberish as, "Pretentious or needlessly obscure language." This is so close to edubabble that the latter term may be described as gibberish in an educational setting. A promising trend may develop from this analysis. There could be "medibabble" for the health care sector, "polibabble" for those in politics and government or "jock-a-babble" for those in the sports field; *see also Edubabble-Characteristics.*

**GOTHIC HORROR** *see Varney the Vampire, Young Adult Gothic Horror.*

**GRAD HUG** Male educators need to practice the grad hug before any potentially misconstrued display of affection in front of hundreds if not thousands of people. It is appropriate to engage in a hug if the female student clearly wishes to share one. However, the man's shoulders should lean forward with arms extended only to reach the girl's upper back. The man's hips should be extended outward and backward so as to not make physical contact. A gentle pat on the shoulder to indicate the end of the embrace is a good idea.

**GRADING STUDENT WORK** There are several locales where grading sheaths of student work is not a sound idea. These include:

    a) on the beach during a particularly windy day;

    b) around a roaring campfire with embers flying about;

    c) lounging poolside as teens practice their belly-flops and cannonballs.

A teacher should also avoid grading papers after a rousing verbal sparring match with a partner, spouse, or teenage son or daughter. Evaluating student work is also not recommended during or after consuming copious amounts of wine and/or beer. Spilling alcohol on the papers will make the work impossible to read and leave a stain that requires explanation; *see also, Homemade Wine.*

**GRAPEVINE - STUDENT** Counselors and principals who want to tap into the high school student grapevine should talk to the woodwork or textiles teacher. When students are engaged in a project, they start to chat with each other. And when they chat with each other, stories unfold. Students become so captivated by fiddling with the project and swapping tales and rumors, they usually forget about the presence of the teacher who is usually flitting about the room with ears open.

**GREASE MONKEYS** Societal trends and new technology create new jobs such as the Gamers. But they eliminate some occupations and certain social groupings as well. In the past there were always students, almost always boys, who loved to tinker with cars. They could be seen in the school's Mechanics shop or in their garage at home, car hood up. The youth could be seen staring at the engine, grease-stained white cloth in hand before diving in to twist bolts or fiddle with hoses. Sometimes the car would appear deformed with giant mag wheels and a power engine accompanying a tiny chassis.

Alas, these "grease monkeys" or "shop jocks" have all but disappeared from schools as cars have become more computerized, technical, and almost robotic; *see also Fortnite.*

**GREAT EXPECTATIONS** Notwithstanding the appropriated use of the Dickensian title, if a student has worked diligently through the public-school years, what is the expected reward? Answer—more of the same at college, technical institute, or university.

**GROUP THINK** Despite the oft-repeated desire to inculcate creative and independent cognition, there are examples from school life when all involved think the same way. Some examples are:

a) the complaining that will occur from the members of a lower-ability English class when the teacher announces that they will be studying a play by Shakespeare. Imagine that, Shakespeare in an English class!

b) the universal positive response from teachers when the principal announces that another non-instructional day has been added to the examination schedule;

c) the pleasure from all when hearing that the wise superintendent has canceled the school day due to foreboding weather;

d) the whining from all when hearing that the moronic superintendent has kept the schools open despite the foreboding weather.

**GUINEA PIG STUDENTS** A program needs to be piloted. A new teaching methodology requires testing. Someone in the district needs to gather some data for a Masters or EdD thesis. So, in essence, the students become the laboratory guinea pigs. No one seems concerned about using the students in this manner. If the program was a bust. If the new teaching methodology did not work. If the thesis parameters were flawed, what does this say about the students' experience? *see also, Doctorate Programs in Education.*

**GUITAR CLASS** Anyone who has taught a beginner guitar class realizes that more than half the period will be taken up by students trying to tune their instruments. The general cacophony of twenty-five inexpert students plunking on strings and twisting the tuning pegs makes achieving any sense of harmonious sound impossible. The experienced guitar teacher cannot be of much help with earplugs jammed into the side of a tortured head; *see also, Orchestral Class.*

# H

**HAIR - MUSICAL** *see Jesus Christ Superstar.*

**HALLWAY MONITORS** Video surveillance cameras have replaced adult hallway supervisors in many high schools. Whether this is more effective in curtailing student misbehavior is debatable. Enterprising teens are more likely to disable the cameras than neutralize the humans. A can of spray paint aimed at a camera lens is more easily accomplished than tying and gagging a human hall monitor; *see also, Drones.*

**HANDBALL** Sometimes referred to as European Handball, this Olympic sport involves movement and coordination similar to basketball without the need to be in the ninety-eighth percentile in height. There are several "foreign" games that should be taught in North American schools and this is one of them. It should also be noted that soccer was once referred to as a "foreign" game.

American teachers should not get too carried away though. Some foreign sports are too violent for litigation-averse US schools. These include Rugby, Aussie Rules Football, and Celtic Hurling. In none of these sports do the players wear padding and the "game" resembles barely organized mayhem to the uninitiated; *see also, Soccer.*

**HANDWRITING** *see Writing-Cursive.*

**HEURISTIC LEARNING** Superb edubabble. The adjective heuristic sounds truly impressive and is three syllables in length. A bonus is that the word is difficult to pronounce and harder to spell. The noun it describes is appropriately commonplace, adding to the mystique of meaning. The actual definition of heuristic learning also lends to the phrase being regarded as excellent edubabble; the placing of a smattering of objects in a location so students can manipulate and utilize the objects with creativity and imagination without adult influence is common-sense simple; *see also, Edubabble-Characteristics (b) (e).*

**HEUTAGOGY** Get ready for some more prime, grade-A edubabble. Heutagogy is instructional practice in which the learning is self-determined both in destination and choice of method. According to heutagogy adherents, knowing how to learn will be a fundamental skill in the future. The teacher acts as a coach, guide, or resource but not the primary source of knowledge. This approach encourages students to find their own problems and questions to answer.

If for some bizarre reason a teacher wishes to win a fantasy pool for edubabble, a phrase such as the following is sure to be a winner, "My methodology has shifted from archaic pedagogy reliant on operant conditioning to a heutagogical approach more aligned with contemporary heuristic learning styles." After hearing such spectacular drivel, any competitors will readily accept defeat knowing they have lost to an edubabble wizard; *see also, Idea Thread Mapper, Journal of Learning Sciences, Pedagogy.*

**HIGH RISE SCHOOLS** The high-rise school is coming to a neighborhood near you. A major thrust of urban renewal is to build residential communities downtown. Thus, the urban core will not continue to be some kind of strange way-station where people visit during the work-day before scurrying off to the suburbs in the evening. Building residences means housing people— and people, especially younger adults, have children. The children need to attend school so these will need to be built. But land is ridiculously expensive in the urban core, making the sprawling one or two-story school design impractical. So, like the residences, the schools will be more than a few storeys in height.

There will be challenges to be sure. Class changes might mean cramped elevators. Fire drills will be interesting. Having the emergency evacuation muster area on a major downtown street blocking the flow of traffic will likely cause a bit of agitation with the driving public, especially with the always-pleasant taxi drivers.

**HOLLOW PROMISES - PARENTS** Adults are just as keen as teens to display dripping sincerity when providing pledges that action will occur when nothing of the sort will actually happen. These include those promising to:

    a) refrain from taking their teen on shopping trips during school days;

    b) institute at least one consequence at home when the teen's school behavior is poor;

    c) cease covering for their teen when the student is truant.

**HOLLOW PROMISES - PRINCIPALS** The opportunity to make all manner of rosy assurances that will only have a passing association with what will likely occur is too good to pass up for a few miscreant principals. A few notable statements are:

    a) "I will have an open-door policy this year,"—Reality is that the office door will be closed ninety percent of the time;

    b) "I will be visiting your classrooms on a regular basis,"—Reality is that the principal will never be seen in the hallways, yet alone in a classroom;

    c) "I will be seeking your input on new school procedures and policies,"—Reality is that teachers will receive a memo outlining the changes.

**HOLLOW PROMISES - STUDENTS** A teacher can hear a great many hollow promises from incorrigible students who have been reprimanded yet never change. These include those promising to:

    a) submit at least one more assignment than the previous term, thus doubling the total;

    b) refrain from power-napping at the back of the room;

    c) attend more than one class a week;

    d) not make any additional hollow promises.

Those few incorrigible students who display such behavior skirt along the line that separates hollow promises from habitual lying. On a positive note, they may possess a unique gift that can lead to a successful political career; *see also, Anti-Educators (e), Congress.*

**HOMEMADE WINE** This glossary is not intended solely as a resource to better understand and confidently engage in edubabble. Hopefully there are valuable hints to make a teaching career more successful and pleasurable. The following is one of those hints; do not bring homemade wine to a staff party, no matter how 'full-bodied" you believe your home-brew to be; *see also, Grading Student Work, Oral Fixation.*

**HOTBEDS OF DISSENT** A base of truth can under-pin a stereotype. That statement has merit when the stereotypical dissenting artist of today is matched with the "unconventional" background of some famous visual artists of the past. The Impressionists were considered radicals at the time. After an 1874 exhibition the group had organized (having been refused other opportunities), they received stinging criticism from the Arts establishment. Monet and Cezanne were particularly scorned. Max Ernst, considered one of the founders of the Dada and surrealist movements of the early 20th century, lived in a *ménage a trois* in 1920's Paris and used controversial Freudian dream images as a stimulus for many of his paintings. Pablo Picasso's family sent him to Madrid to attend Art school when he was sixteen, but he stopped attending.

Is the high school Art room the favored space for teenage malcontents or is that "honor" spread out among various areas of the school? Do those students who lean toward Art really see the world differently than other people? Is there really such a trait as a volatile artistic temperament?

Be tactful if you ask the Art teacher these questions, especially the latter one! *see also, New Art Form, Romantic Poets, Website Project.*

**HUMAN RESOURCES DEPARTMENT** Just as citizens have become taxpayers and sports stars, team "assets," workers such as teachers have become "resources." This makes these people akin to a textbook, laptop computer, or atlas.

# I

**ICON** Putting the tech definition of an icon as a computer symbol to the side, an alternative definition of an icon is a revered person who represents the essential characteristics of a group. It appears that most professions have such people. Business people may see Henry Ford as an icon of the industrial age and Bill Gates as one for the new era of computer technology. Science has numerous icons, Albert Einstein and Isaac Newton being two. Nursing has Florence Nightingale and doctors' Jonas Salk. Politicians of every stripe would likely include Nelson Mandela.

Who are the icons of public education? As a quick example of action research, gather ten teacher colleagues together, ask for five icons of public education, then analyze the results; *see also, Mason.*

**IDEA THREAD MAPPER** According to the Center for Innovative Research in Cyberlearning (CIRCL) an Idea Thread Mapper is explained as, "Beyond micro-level representations of ideas in online discourse as postings and build-ons, ITM uses an idea thread to represent a line of inquiry and clusters of idea threads to represent community-wide advances in a whole initiative."

After that explanatory gem, what more needs to be said? *see also, Heutagogy, Journal of Learning Sciences, Monks of the Digital Age, Oligarchs in Education (c).*

**IDIOMS** While teenagers should be able to understand idioms, there may be a few adolescent athletes who still reside in a purely literal world and may take the following common sports phrases to heart:

    a) "Take one for the team,"—this promotes locker room theft;

    b) "Leave nothing out there,"—this too encourages thievery but of articles left lying around the field;

    c) "Hit the showers,"—this suggests physical assault on inanimate objects that can cause hand injury;

    d) "Give more than 100%,"—this causes confusion among the arithmetically challenged and thus could increase student stress and anxiety.

**IGEN** Goodbye (finally) to the Boomer generation. Move over Millennials. The iGen is coming to a teachers' lounge near you. According to *Forbes*, the generation born between 1995 and the mid-2000s comprises 25% of the US population. This makes this generation larger than the Millennials and the Boomers. Early members of the iGen have already graduated from university. A few may have been appointed to their first teaching jobs.

As the first generation to have little or no memory of the 9/11 terrorist attacks and be the first to have used the internet their entire lives, it will be interesting to see how they shape the education of the future. No worries here; *see also, Generation Z, Job Security.*

**IMAGE - PROFESSORIAL** There are very few ways for men to appear professorial in contemporary high schools. Male teachers used to be able to display their academic chops by toting a briefcase or smoking a pipe. Elbow patches on a rumpled Harris Tweed sportscoat were a nice touch. For good or bad, these accoutrements of academia life have all but disappeared. It is difficult to have a scholarly affectation when adorning oneself with what the uneducated masses wear—khakis, polo shirts, and loafers; *see also, Endangered Species-Teachers (a), Khakis.*

**IMPROVISATION** There have been very few teachers who have not walked into a classroom unprepared for a lesson or an entire day at least a few times in a career. When that occurs, improv skills need to come to the fore. While it is not wise to make a habit of using them too often, these skills can come in very handy and should be part of every teacher's tool kit. If one gets really adept at improv there may be some question about the teacher's commitment to planning; *see also, Acting, Mishaps of Classroom Technology.*

**INCREMENTS** Levels, steps, increments—whatever the laddering of teacher pay is called, the scale essentially assumes that a person becomes a better teacher as more experience is gained. After all, why would a teacher with the same qualifications with eight years experience receive a markedly higher salary than a colleague with two years experience? Though there is a wide variance across North America, in some jurisdictions there is a ten-year or more increment scale, a kind of uber-lengthy apprenticeship system.

Interestingly, few have asked if the employer's expectations for competency are the same for the second-year teacher as they are for the teacher with eight year's experience. One would have to assume that the expectations are identical since few School Boards would want to admit to parents that the second-year professional teaching their teen is less competent that the eight-year veteran instructing the sibling. And if the qualifications and competency are the same, why the gap in pay?

**INFORMATION SCIENCE** *see Library Science.*

**INKLINGS (THE)** One of the secondary reasons for this glossary is to provide the teachers who bother to read it with trifles and trivia related to teaching. This helps them sound knowledgeable in the teachers' lounge at recess and lunch as well as at the watering hole on Friday afternoons.

While the Inklings may sound like an early 1960s "doo-wop" group wearing thin ties and showcasing smooth moves, it was an informal literary group in Oxford between the two world wars. The group met in a pub, where else? Most importantly for teachers, two of the members were J.R.R. Tolkien and C.S. Lewis. Their writings, particularly, *The Hobbit* and *The Lord of the Rings* (Tolkien) and *The Chronicles of Narnia* (Lewis) are classics; *see also, Know–It–All Colleague.*

**INPUT ON BUDGET** The vast portion of a school district's budget is comprised of wages and salaries, most of which are set by various collective agreements. Despite this, school board members, being community-based politicians, love to engage the public with input sessions about the budget even if they don't really understand it themselves. This enables the most vocal special-interest parents to come to the fore, arguing for what benefits their child—more sports for those with athletic teens, more fine arts for those musically or theatrically inclined, more paraprofessionals for those with special needs. The unions, unable to discuss any reductions to their ranks, lobby against the one group they can shoot at, that being supervisors. With such parental and union narrowness, is there any wonder that little comes of such sessions? *see also, Interest Groups.*

**INSTRUCTIONAL SCAFFOLDING** This is an excellent example of edubabble and owes its name from the artifice that provides successive levels of support to workers as they climb higher on a construction site. As the teacher builds the learning supports, the student gradually becomes a more independent learner. For many non-educators this would seem common-sensical as a teaching strategy, though they may miss how difficult it is to do effectively with thirty students in a class. For teachers, it is great edubabble since it is an impressively convoluted title which in essence can be summarized as, "I do it, we do it, you do it."

**INTELLIGENCE TESTING – MASSES** There had to be some method for determining who should lead and who should follow when tens of thousands of young men were suddenly lining up at US army recruitment centers when the country entered World War I (two and a half years after the war began). Intelligence tests that had been developed in France were "Americanized." These Stanford-Binet IQ tests provided the answer, or so it was believed at the time. The Alpha variety was a written test. The Beta version was a series of pictures for recruits who were illiterate or who did not speak English. Over two million tests were administered. Whether the mass IQ testing was helpful in achieving the military goals is debatable. No matter, the practice was later enthusiastically pursued in public education; *see also, One Hundred Thirty-Two.*

**INTEREST GROUPS** Special interest groups love education as much as bears love honeypots. Educators are always asking for input on how schools should operate, thus making the opportunity to push a specific agenda readily available. There is parent participation on various committees, boring work to be sure but opportunity nevertheless to further champion a specific cause. To make matters even better, it is very easy to acquire a semblance of importance. There are school parent councils and specialty parent councils for programs such as music or sports. There are district-wide parent groups with the main criteria for being selected to the executive is that a person sticks up a hand when no one else does. Once a person is known as a "parent leader" access is granted to all the input opportunities a school or district provides; *see also, Input on Budget.*

**INTERNATIONAL SCHOOLS** There is an army of teachers flitting about the globe teaching in one private international school after another. The students are usually the children of business people working overseas. The funds provided to the school are often as much as three times the amount provided to public schools in the United States or Canada. It is no wonder that once on the international circuit relatively few of these teachers return home until they are ready to retire.

**INTERRUPTING** A teacher really cannot blame students for interrupting. Even a casual observance of any "news panel" will reveal that the talking heads never stop punctuating the conversation with gems of self-declared wisdom. Even the so-called moderator spends an inordinate amount of time interrupting. The behavior of most of these panelists would not be tolerated for long in a classroom. The perpetrators would be sent to the hallway for their inability to listen respectfully to another person's point of view; *see also, Brevity is the Soul of Wit, Congress, Journalism, Manners-Teaching Of.*

**IN THE GYM** PE teachers may find the following difficult to comprehend since they were good athletes when they were in school. One reason that student enrolment in PE suffers a dramatic drop once it is an elective is the public display of incompetence that students suffer when they are poor at whatever task is at hand. If a student is a poor reader in an English class, he or she can usually find ways to hide the weakness from public display. Few English teachers would force a student who is a very poor reader to read aloud. If a student does not have a clue in Math class there are only a few occasions where that becomes public knowledge, most likely when receiving a mark on a test.

In a Gym class, the inability to catch a ball, or hit the birdie, or shoot a basket, is on display for all to see. Since the student's public ineptitude will go on and on, is it any wonder that the student will abandon the class at the first opportunity? *see also, Ipsative Assessment, Jell-O, What Were They Thinking? (b), Yoga.*

**INTO THE FUTURE - REALITY** Primary teachers may have solid predictions about their students in the future. But aside from hearsay, the odd Facebook connection, or newspaper article, they do not have a great deal of opportunity to gauge the accuracy of their prophetic prowess.

On the other hand, high school teachers have a unique opportunity to test the accuracy of their predictions about their student's futures by attending a school reunion. The twentieth homecoming social provides a relatively accurate reading since the former students are in their late thirties and thus true adults.

When attending a reunion, the teacher is likely to feel a little uneasy, assuming, of course, that he or she cannot share ribald stories of inebriation and petty vandalism with former students. The teacher may find that the mouthy, know-it-all disruptor from years ago is now a small city mayor who has made a fortune in real estate. The bullied female science geek may be running a break-through medical software business. The star jock might be a janitor at her company.

**IPSATIVE ASSESSEMENT** Check the boxes for good edubabble. The adjective ipsative has three syllables and describes a relatively simple noun, assessment. Despite sounding impressively complex and sophisticated, the essence of the term is relatively simple. Ipsative assessment is based on a comparison between the individual's current performance and that achieved in the past, thus differing from normative assessment which compares performance to established norms. This form of assessment might be beneficial in PE classes where individuals, due to body type or size, lung capacity, or naturally poor motor skills, cannot reach a normed benchmark; *see also, Edubabble-Characteristics, In the Gym.*

# J

**JAVERT AND VALJEAN** Questions of commitment versus fanaticism, justice as distinct from law, equal as opposed to special treatment; these are the essence of ethical and moral dilemmas faced by these fictional characters that are as relevant today as they were when Victor Hugo wrote *Les Misérables* in the 1840s. With political, business, and entertainment leaders seemingly displaying increasingly questionable ethical behavior, should schools begin to focus more on the teaching of ethics and morals? Will such a move be co-opted by special interest groups on each of the extreme right and left of the political spectrum? The answer to the latter question is, unfortunately, probably; *see also, Ethical Standards.*

**JELL-O** There is little difference between this substance (whatever it really is) and the muscle tone of the young stereotypical gamers and related techno-nuts who sit for hour upon hour in their parent's basement glued to a monitor. Their muscles atrophy and the eyes resemble those of moles, their closest relation in the animal kingdom. These students could use a double-dose of PE classes but are likely to concoct a strategy to avoid the gym at all costs; *see also, Baseball, Fortnite, In the Gym, Screen Addicts, What Were They Thinking? (b), World Cup of Fortnite, Yoga.*

**JESUS CHRIST SUPERSTAR** What was once controversial becomes accepted. Marijuana, the evil weed, is legal in some states and across Canada. Teaching evolution in Tennessee was deemed illegal until the Butler Act was repealed in 1967, the same year the US Supreme Court ruled that state laws banning interracial marriage were unconstitutional.

The 1970 rock opera *Jesus Christ Superstar* offended a fair number of people when it was released as a record album and soon after as a theatrical production. Controversial at the time, it is now a staple high school production. Even *Hair* which opened on Broadway in 1968 and was far more controversial than *Jesus Christ Superstar,* is performed as a high school musical, though as a somewhat sanitized version. Students performing in these shows today may wonder why their glassy-eyed grandparents want to attend night-after-night; *see also, Gateway Drug, Rap Music.*

**JITTERY SPEAKERS** It would seem logical to assume that a group of people who spend their working day talking in front of teens would find little trouble speaking to an adult audience. That, however, is not the case. A surprisingly high percentage of teachers would rather sit in a dentist chair and have a root canal than speak in front of adults. Why the jitters when these teachers spend all their working day in front of people? Their response is usually akin to, "That's different," as if that is a full and logical explanation.

**JOAN OF ARC** The original cross-dressing teen, Joan of Arc traveled as a boy to avoid the authorities. This young woman, supposedly treasonous and a heretic, was put on trial when nineteen years of age. An additional charge was cross-dressing. She was later canonized by the Catholic Church; *see also, Genderqueer.*

**JOB INTERVIEW** *see Questions in Interviews–Strategy One, Questions in Interviews–Strategy Two.*

**JOB SECURITY** E-Learning, distributed learning, distance learning, computer-assisted learning, asynchronous learning, artificial intelligence—will these tech-laden approaches have lasting impact on the traditional educational model of a teacher standing in front of a group of students? Will the predictions of the demise of human beings as teachers be similar to the predictions of how 1950s and 60s television was going to revolutionize the way schools operated and how their teachers worked? Not much really changed that time. Will it on this occasion? *see also, iGen.*

**JOB SHADOWING** What a great idea! Have students shadow an adult (parent, aunt, uncle) while the person is on the job. This works well for some occupations such as teacher, receptionist, retail worker, editor, waitperson in a restaurant, and veterinarian, to name a few. It does not work so well if the adult in question is a brain surgeon, prison guard, or undercover police officer. In addition, some occupations may not be appropriate for youth to be directly exposed to such as mob boss, loan shark, ambulance-chasing lawyer, or hedge-fund manager.

**JOE CLARK** There are not many public-school educators who make the front cover of *Time Magazine* but Joe Clark did. He was the principal of Eastside High School in New Jersey from 1982 to 1991. He liked to carry a baseball bat and bullhorn while striding through the hallways encouraging, cajoling, or berating students. He locked the school doors to keep the thugs out but made safe exit for students difficult in an emergency. He suspended hundreds of students and had a movie based on his time at the school, *Lean on Me* starring Morgan Freeman. Test scores did rise slightly during his tenure but that may have been because he rid the school of delinquent students, many of whom were not likely to be academic stars. Controversial, he was an educational mirror for the Reagan age, seen either as a shining star or dangerous demagogue of school leadership. After Eastside, Clark worked in a juvenile delinquent facility.

The reader is left to ponder how a principal would need to behave in order to be a leadership example in the Trump era; *see also, Anti–Educators–Leaders (a), Journalism.*

**JOLT OF CAFFEINE** Students are drinking more coffee and at a younger age. They have likely discovered that when it comes to getting that jolt of caffeine in the morning, coffee punts soft drinks into the minor leagues. According to the Center for Science in the Public Interest, leading the caffeine pack are the 20 oz. Starbucks Blonde Roast and the Dunkin Donuts 20 oz. Turbo Shot coming in at 475 and 398 milligrams of caffeine respectively.

In comparison, the top two sodas, 20 oz Pepsi zero sugar and 20 oz. Mountain Dew have a paltry 115 and 91 milligrams of caffeine, truly pathetic on the jolt scale. Even the Red Bull Energy drink, which, according to their ad, "gives you wings," has a meager 80 milligrams of caffeine in an 8 oz. serving.

**JOURNALISM** Pity the journalism teacher attempting to foster objectivity and ethical standards in an era of "fake news" and "alternate facts." Everyone with an ax to grind has a website. Anyone can jump into the Twitter "dialogue." American TV "news" networks are little more than propaganda agencies for a defined political agenda; *see also, Anti–Educators–Leaders (e), Ethical Standards, Interrupting, Smoke Pit, Talking Heads, Weapons of Mass Distortion.*

**JOURNAL OF LEARNING SCIENCES** The Learning Sciences is a new field so the Journal must be working hard to establish an audience. With a 2018 article entitled "Co-organizing the Collective Journey of Inquiry with Idea Thread Mapper," it is not likely to be on the stand at the grocery store check-out line. It is not likely to be found in the hands of many teachers either, which is a strange fate for a periodical dedicated to learning; *see also, Heutagogy, Idea Thread Mapper, Oligarchs in Education (c), Situated Learning.*

**JUNE/JULY** No matter how much a teacher enjoys the job, June, the end of the school year (at least in most districts) brings excitement about what July will bring— reading trashy novels, traveling at peak-price times, and catching up on illnesses one did not have time for during the school year.

**JUNK** Teachers are surrounded by junk. There is junk food in the school's vending machines. Their mail boxes are filled with junk mail. Junk theories of learning are foisted on them with regularity. Schools collect all manner of material and furniture and never throw anything out. Therefore, the school's storage area is always crammed with . . . junk.

**JUUL** There are occasions when companies make a tremendous amount of money catering to young people, sometimes due to fortunate circumstance, sometimes because of dubious methods, and sometimes both simultaneously. Juul is one such company.

According to the 2017 National Youth Survey, smoking among high school students decreased 73% from 2000 to 2017. Societal change, and yes, teacher leadership in health-related courses, contributed to this success.

Originally touted as a good route to stop smoking, e-cigarettes have recently become more prevalent. Juul has taken this trend to a new level with an astounding market share of over 70% among vaping teens. Resembling a USB flash drive, the small size, less smoke than competitors, and enticing flavors makes it the "go to" device. The product has the dubious distinction of helping to reverse the downward trend in connecting teens with nicotine. Some individual pods of Juul contain almost as much nicotine as an entire package of regular cigarettes. A new generation of nicotine-addicted teens may have arrived, rekindling another challenge to the schools to correct the results of corporate excess; *see also, David and Goliath, Love That Nicotine, Smoke Pit.*

# K

**KALE** In the 1990s this lettuce-like vegetable became well known in North America. However, this "new superfood" has been grown in the Mediterranean region for thousands of years. The culinary correct brigade will no doubt demand that it be used in school cafeterias, if they have not done so already. But twenty years of popularity for any "foreign" food can be a long time in North America. School cafeteria programs may want to get ahead of the curve and emphasize bok choy and lentils over kale and quinoa; *see also, Culinary Correctness, Quinoa, Vending Machines.*

**KELLER, HELEN** If teachers need an adrenaline shot about the need to educate those with learning challenges and the impact a teacher can have, the story of hearing and visually challenged Helen Keller and her teacher, Anne Sullivan is a good place to start. Sullivan, visually impaired herself, was hired as Keller's teacher when she was twenty and Keller seven, eventually becoming governess and later a companion-friend to Keller. The 1957 play *The Miracle Worker* is based in Keller's story. The 1962 movie version starred Anne Bancroft as teacher Sullivan and Patty Duke as Keller. Both actors won Academy Awards for their performances.

**KEYNOTE - BUSINESS PERSON'S LUNCH** A teacher giving a talk to a local business person's lunch may be met with the stereotypical comment about teaching being an "easy" 9-3:00 job with "lots of holidays." The natural tendency is to dispute that claim with a contrary point of view, focusing on the challenges of the occupation and likely sounding a tad defensive. This is the type of response the audience expects.

An interesting twist might be to surprise everyone by giving wholehearted agreement that teaching is indeed a breeze of a job. This type of sardonic reply could include the following steps:

a) State, "Yes, you are correct. Teaching is the slackest job on the planet and I get oodles of holiday time";

b) Mock with, "You guys really missed the boat on not going into education when you had the chance. What were you thinking?"

c) Lean forward and offer a twisted smile. Give a little shrug as if you can't help it if you were clever in your career choice and the audience was a pack of dim-witted fools for not hopping on such a gravy train;

d) Enjoy the stunned silence.

**KHAKIS** These pants are the official uniform of the male teacher league; *see also, Image-Professorial.*

**KICKBACKS** This term has an unsavory tinge describing an "exchange of favors." Any educators engaging in such dubious activity should use the more gentle, officious-sounding, quid-pro-quo; *see also, Letters of Reference (1), Quid-Pro-Quo.*

**KILOMETER** In the United States only those teaching science or coaching track events know about this logical measure of distance as evidenced by:

   a) a kilometer is 1,000 meters. A mile is 1,760 yards;
   b) a meter is 100 centimeters. A yard is 36 inches;
   c) A foot is 12 inches. There are 5,280 feet in a mile. There is no equivalent for a foot in metric measurement.

Hmm, measured distance based on units of 10 used consistently, or a 12-1 (inches to feet), 3-1 (feet to yards), and 1,760-1 (yards to miles)? Which system makes more sense? *see also, Miles and Inches.*

**KINESTHETIC/TACTILE LEARNING** Though the vast majority of teachers are not likely to be too concerned with the supposed differences between kinesthetic and tactile learning, some education theorists are. Some regard kinesthetic and tactile learning as one and the same. Others believe kinesthetic learning involves the student moving large muscles and tactile learning the sensation of touch on the skin. The debate will no doubt continue to rage among the sixteen people in the country who actually care, none of whom are teachers; *see also, Quibble (2)*.

**KLEENEX BOX** A teacher may be fortunate and not have a colleague who is a member of the grouser group. However, it is more likely there will be at least one chronic complainer who will be focusing on poor student behavior generally and one or two "problem" students in particular. This grumbler seems to believe that removing the one or two troublemakers will ensure peace and harmony. The other teachers know better. The complainer will always grouse about the, "Worst kid in the school." If that student leaves the school, a new "worst kid" will automatically pop up, just like a Kleenex tissue pulled from the box; *see also, Crisis Junkies, Deadline, Meeting Behavior-Teachers (e), Toxicity Pit*.

**KLINGON** Schools have not started to teach this language, yet. In the 1980s Star Trek creator Gene Roddenberry wanted a "real" Klingon language, so linguist Marc Okrand was hired and he created a verbal and written language. It is not an easy language to learn nor should it be. Klingons are (were?) a difficult species. Besides the fictitious nerds on *The Big Bang Theory* babbling on in Klingon, Wikipedia claims that there are about a dozen humans who are fluent in Klingon. This makes the language about as well used as Latin outside the Catholic Church; *see also, Periodic Table of the Elements*.

**KNITTING** How retro can a program be? How about an activity that is good for developing fine motor skills that can lead to thumb-tapping prowess while allowing the student to conduct a conversation with others at the same time! This sounds promising as a relaxing activity to calm the hormonal beast forever lurking in early-adolescent bodies. Before a school introduces such a crafts-oriented elective, beware that early teens can make weapons out of virtually anything. Knitting needles could be handy as mini-swords in a swashbuckling duel or for simply jabbing an adversary; *see also, Archery, Field Events, Thumb Tapping, Xylophone (c).*

**KNOW-IT-ALL COLLEAGUE** You have to be of a certain age to remember the television show *Cheers* and one of its more colorful characters, know-it-all, Cliff Clavin. Of course, fiction is especially effective when it closely reflects reality. Most workplaces have at least one pompous Cliff Clavin mouthing off in the lunch room about every topic imaginable. Schools are more likely to have as many, or more, Clavins than other workplaces. Teachers are, for the most part, verbal. They are also, on average, intelligent. And they spend their day dispensing knowledge. This trifactor background can make a dangerous breeding ground for Clavin-like behavior; *see also, Meeting Behavior-Teachers (a), Red School House, White Noise (a), Yellow School Bus.*

**KRYPTON** The origin-of-Superman creators must have been paying attention in their Science class since

Krypton is an earthly element with an Atomic number of 36. There is no evidence that the ability to fly results from copious consumption of the element; *see also, Periodic Table of the Elements.*

**K (SILENT LETTER)** Occasionally laziness and curiosity can make strange bedfellows. English teachers are expected to teach spelling. This is not easy to do since the English language has origins in a mish-mash of Greek, Latin, German, French, Celtic, and Nordic languages, as well as just about any other group who visited, traded with, or invaded, the British Isles.

Sooner of later, a student who is desirous of cutting corners or is truly curious will ask a question such as, "Why do I have to write the K letter in knit and knight and knee when the word would sound the same without it? Isn't writing the K a waste of time?"

This is a good question and one a teacher should be prepared to answer. "Be quiet and do your work," does not qualify as an enlightened response; *see also, Zee to Zed.*

# L

**LANGUAGE ACQUISITION - TEACHERS** One of the benefits of being a high school teacher is the opportunity to pick up new language skills courtesy of the teenage students. In previous years, dude, sweet, or no worries, could occasionally find their way into a teacher's vocabulary. Recently it could be goat (greatest of all time), squad, fam or peep for a friendship group, or gucci for something good or cool. The feeling in the teachers' lounge on the last day of school is so goat that the squad is looking for a gucci time; *see also, June/July, Lit, Obscenity and Profanity.*

**LASER EYES** Firing laser eyes at a misbehaving student is an effective means of curbing undesirable behavior. Unfortunately, the technique does not have the same impact with adults. Doing the same at a conference session when the presenter is yakking on about some inane idea rarely works. Audience connectivity is not a high priority with workshop presenters.

Firing laser eyes at a principal in full-flight monologue at a teacher meeting will probably ruffle some peacock feathers. This will likely result in an intimate "chat" with the boss with or without the presence of the union rep. A claim could be made that your unblinking, staring eyes were a sign of being enthralled at the wisdom being presented to you. Unfortunately, only a truly dim-wit of a principal would buy that story; *see also, Monologue.*

**LATERAL THINKING** The ability to use an indirect, creative approach to find new and alternate solutions is regarded by most teachers as a valuable skill. While this may be true in the classroom, it is rarely seen at the negotiating table when hashing out details for new collective agreements in the Education sector; *see also, Meeting Behavior-Teachers (f), Thinking.*

**LEADING ROLES** Choosing actors for a high school musical production can be difficult. There are usually far more girls than boys competing for leading roles. If a director has a very strong-voiced male of at least average size, then *Fiddler on the Roof* may be a good choice since there is a natural Tevye. *Jesus Christ Superstar* has only one female lead and even with double-casting, satisfying the number of girls competing for the Mary Magdalene part is difficult.

Borrowing from Shakespeare only in reverse, the solution is to cast girls in male roles. It can work for the Judas Iscariot part in *Superstar*. It does not fit so well for the Kenickie role in *Grease* or the Conrad Birdie character in *Bye Bye Birdie*, unless the teacher-director wishes to throw gender completely out the window and be at the forefront of a new age in school productions; *see also, Auditions, Genderqueer, Jesus Christ Superstar.*

**LEARNER-CENTERED CLASSROOM** This contemporary term is surprisingly straightforward, describing a classroom that is not teacher-centered. In addition, the term actually means what it says. These two points alone make it relatively poor edubabble; *see also, Edubabble-Characteristics.*

**LEARNING COMMONS** Anyone who has watched a silent movie and compared it to today's special effects blockbusters will attest that movies have changed. Yet they still retain the same term, movie. Today's airplanes and cars bear little resemblance to those of the 1930s though they have retained their original terms. But in Education there seems to be a need to tack on a new name when changes occur to a program or facility. Hence the rigid, structured, quiet library of the past is now a Learning Commons with a newly appropriate buzz of learner activity, flexible chairs, bean-bag furniture, and a variety of learning materials at hand; *see also, FACSE, Quibble (1).*

**LECTURE METHOD** Using this style as a sole method of teaching has definitely gone out of vogue and for good reason. Why should a student be forced to listen to a teacher dispensing information when an internet scan will find the same material much quicker and more concisely? Given the traditions of university-level teaching, the lecture hall facilities, the ridiculously large class sizes at the undergraduate level, and yes, the egos of some professors, it is unlikely that the lecture method will be leaving the staid halls of academia anytime soon; *see also, Talking Heads.*

## LETTERS OF REFERENCE

1. Those teaching seniors in "academic" areas can be swamped with requests for supporting letters as their students prepare for the paper-chase of college and university admissions. Ignore any temptation to use the same letter for ten students or to garner a little "reward" for your efforts. The kickback hill is steep. Once a person starts on the moral slide downward it is tough to climb back to the ethical even-ground; *see also, Kickbacks, Quid-Pro-Quo.*

2. Teachers requesting a reference from a principal usually ask one question, "Can I include you as a reference?" However, there should be an additional query, "Will it be a positive one?"

**LIBRARY SCIENCE** Most trained librarians hold a university degree in Library Science (sometimes referred to as Information Science or even Library and Information Science). The Encyclopedia Britannica, in a mercifully brief description, defines Library Science as,

"The principles and practices of library operation and administration, and their study." While an important role to be sure, it remains unclear how such work is termed a science; *see also FACSE, Management Science, Names and Titles–Science.*

**LIMERICK** Anyone teaching the limerick style of verse to high school students is asking for trouble since the verses are often of a bawdy nature beyond that which classroom decorum would normally allow; *see also, Nantucket, Obscenity and Profanity.*

**LIT** Knowledge of contemporary teen slang can be useful in extolling the virtues of an academic subject. This 2019-20 teen expression for amazing or awesome, wild, or exciting, has potential to be linked to an English lesson promoting literature; *see also, Language Acquisition–Teachers.*

**LOCKERS** A high school teacher looking for an interesting distraction from preparing lessons and filling out administrivia might consider taking a peek inside a student locker, with student permission of course. Just as checking credit card receipts gives marketers an interesting perspective on the demographics of the card holder, the detritus of the locker provides a succinct snapshot of the teen's life. There may be a poster of a muscled young man or a well-endowed young woman pinned to the door, revealing taste in the opposite or same gender. There is the likelihood of potato chip and chocolate bar wrappers strewn about, providing clues as to food preferences. The books stored on a shelf will reflect the classes the teen is enrolled in, indicating future educational plans. Used paint brushes, soiled athletic clothing, or sheet music ripped from a book are good indications of the student's interests.

If a teacher becomes adept at perusing trash to ascertain the base demographics for a product or policy, there is plenty of work outside of teaching for selling a product or marketing a politician; *see also, Attention Economy.*

**LOSING SEASONS** It can be argued that extra-curricular sports are too dominant in many high schools. Only the truly naïve would believe that winning and losing is a distant second to participation and exercise in many coach's minds. Losing seasons can be a grind for coach, players, and parents. Even the principal is impacted, deprived of the chance for vicarious basking in the PR limelight should the team perform well. The following omens are examples of bad news in each of most school's three main sports:

a) in baseball, the new coach finds that the supposedly ace pitcher had an 8.92 ERA the previous season; *see also, Baseball;*

b) in football, the coach discovers that the only quarterback who can accurately throw the ball more than ten yards is red-green color blind, and the school uniform is green with red trim; *see also, Quarterback;*

c) in basketball, the team's starting center is four inches shorter than the average height of the starting guards playing on the other teams in the league; *see also, Recruiting, Economies of Scale.*

**LOVE THAT NICOTINE** One has to be bordering on ancient to recall the hazy days of smoking in the teachers' lounge. In response to complaints, the smokers were banished to separate rooms, usually a space not unlike an unused janitorial closet. When the door opened at the end of the break, a dense shroud of smoke filled the school hallway, leaving students with little doubt as to what was occurring behind the closed doors. The skin, hair, and clothes of the four teachers who had managed to smoke two cigarettes each during a ten-minute break smelled worse than a week-old unemptied ashtray. Most of the students in their classes wanted to sit at the rear of the room as far away from the teacher desk as possible. Now these nicotine-addicted teachers are exiled from the building entirely and either drive around the nearby streets or join the students in the smoke pit where, as the adult interloper, they are made to feel uneasy at best; *see also, Juul, Smoke Pit, What Were They Thinking (a)?*

**LYING** Since education is a "soft" enterprise that values gentle cooperation, teachers can become very adept at using euphemisms. When a student is a habitual liar and the teacher needs to convey such behavior to parents who will not react well to the direct approach,

the following are some creative explanations. Describe
the student as:

a) Working diligently to differentiate between
fantasy and reality;

b) Inhabiting a fascinating world created by intensely
personal interpretation;

c) Becoming aware of the likely consequences of
his/her actions and taking creative steps to avoid
such unpleasantness;

d) Willing to allow others to take responsibility; *see
also, Hollow Promises-Students.*

# M

**MANAGEMENT SCIENCE** F.W. Taylor is generally regarded as the founder of the Scientific Management movement which focused on the systematic analysis of workflow to improve efficiency. Some believed the concepts to be obsolete by the 1930s. But the key points remain in contemporary education bureaucracies with the strict division of labor, high level of managerial control, and continued cost accounting. A partial reason for the long lifespan of the managerial style may be the current fascination in education with tacking the term "science" onto as many activities as possible. This makes Management "Science" particularly appealing; *see also, FACSE, Journal of the Learning Sciences, Library Science, Names and Titles-Science.*

**MANNERS - TEACHING OF** In a time long ago, most students were taught at least a minimum level of manners by their parents, leaving the teacher role to be one of reinforcing and reminding students what was taught at home. There appears to be somewhat of a breakdown in the transmission of what was once referred to as manners. It is not unusual for teachers to spend time reminding students not to yawn without putting a hand over their mouth, refrain from chewing with their mouths open, or constantly interrupting a person who is speaking. Among many teens, the use of profanity has morphed from occasional blurting to the "go to" choice of adjectives and nouns.

Schools have always been expected to step in to fill the gaping holes in society so it should not be much of a surprise that the teaching of manners is becoming more and more common. Given the behavior of certain political, financial, and media leaders, the burden to fill in another societal gap and begin teaching ethics will likely follow; *see also, Congress, Digital Citizenship, Ethical Standards, F-Bomb, Interrupting, Journalism, Yawning.*

**MARCHING BANDS** This genre of music is popular in US high schools but has not caught on in the schools of many other countries. The uniforms, straight out of an 18th century European duchy or 20th century Disneyland, may be a reason. Additionally, other countries, sports-crazy though they may be, do not have high school spectacles that resemble American football which is a mainstay for this form of music. Some other quirks of marching bands are:

  a) the limitations on musicality—the marching musician is tromping about, striving to keep in the same strut with the others, an expectation likely even more important than any skill playing the instrument at-hand;

b) the less-than-ideal venue—football fields or paved streets are not as acoustically sensitive as concert halls so does anyone really notice the level of musicality?

c) the relative musical ignorance of the audience— the people lining the streets at a parade or the seats at a football game are not likely to be a discriminating audience;

*see also, Mason.*

**MARIJUANA** *see Gateway Drug, Weed, Zoned Out.*

**MASON, LOWELL** This person has had an impact on education though he is little known outside music circles. Mr. Mason is credited with founding music education in American schools in the 1840-1870 period; *see also, Balanced Band, Euphonium, Icon, Marching Bands.*

**MBWA** Part of the pop management craze of the 1990's, MBWA stood for Management by Walking Around. This led some principals to wander about their schools, not really doing anything except "keeping in touch" with teachers and students. Holding a pencil or pen in hand and having a small notebook handy was a nice touch. People might think something would actually happen if the boss took written notes of a situation being observed or discussed.

Contemporary texting devices are clearly an upgrade on the pencil and notebooks of the past. However, since everyone has a cellphone and is busy tapping away, the luster of the boss nodding with understanding while stabbing at buttons becomes less shiny. The principal may be scanning the scores from yesterday's football games or checking the market value of the stocks recently purchased.

**MEETING BEHAVIOR - TEACHERS** Behavior in meetings is a fascinating subject not well appreciated by the majority of those sitting through them. If a person's behavior is not aligned with one of the categories listed below, then acting as a spectator and categorizing the comments and body language of colleagues can make a tedious meeting much more interesting. The main categories of teacher meeting behavior are:

a) The Yapper—constantly having something to say about everything. Lack of knowledge or insight does not prevent the yapper from what he/she does best, yap; *see also, Know-It-All Colleague;*

b) The Snoozer—flipping between quick power shut-downs to full fledged snoozing, this person is often the most refreshed at the end of a lengthy and particularly boring meeting; *see also, Weed;*

c) The Enthusiast—for this person, everything discussed is exciting and energizing. There are several colleagues who may begin a search for the metaphorical electrical outlet in order to cut the power source to the enthusiast;

d) The Suck-Up—one good way to ingratiate yourself with the principal is to agree with everything being presented, either verbally or by an energetic nod of the head. This person can encounter neck problems later in life; *see also, Monologue;*

e) The Grouch—adept at alternating between scrunching the face and rolling the eyes upward, the grouch never has a good word to say about anything. Not normally the most popular colleague; *see also, Deadline, Kleenex Box, Toxicity Pit;*

f) The Unionist—for this participant, everything is about collective bargaining and the perceived chasm between management and the union members. Washing coffee cups, toilet paper in the restroom, the decibel level of the bell, the use of the public-address system, and much, much more, are matters seen through the lens of collective bargaining; *see also, Lateral Thinking;*

g) The Silent Majority—most of these people just want the meeting to end so they can get on with more important matters, like grading student work, planning their lessons, and assisting students. They would love to attend meetings where the first six participant styles listed (a-f) are not present but they realize that has yet to occur in any meeting involving more than ten teachers.

**META-COGNITION** When a teenager in a classroom provides a particular gem of insight, a teacher may ask, "An excellent point, how did you come up with that?" Unless the student has been taught basic meta-cognition strategies to develop an awareness of how she or he learns and thinks, the most likely response from the teen is a shoulder shrug and a quick, "I dunno"; *see also, Thinking.*

**MICKEY MOUSE** Some pundits note the "new" trend of merging Art with technology, as evidenced by the visual creativity found in video games. Some schools have altered STEM programs to STEAM (Science, Technology, Engineering, Arts and Mathematics) in response to the importance artistic creativity can bring to the technological forefront.

This is not as new a trend as one may believe. In 1928 Disney's Mickey Mouse made his distributed film debut (*Steamboat Willie*). While it was not the first cartoon to feature a soundtrack, it did synchronize it to the animation, linking this type of sound technology to Art for the first time. Four years later Disney introduced full color three-strip technicolor.

High schools have already adapted to the modern connections between Art and technology. Graphic Arts and Graphic Design courses are far different today than they were two decades ago. Game Design courses are beginning to pop up in high schools and students will be creating video animation much more sophisticated than the films that featured the famous mouse; *see also, New Art Form, Website Project.*

**MILES AND INCHES** American Science and Geography teachers and their students are at a distinct disadvantage when it comes to understanding international measurement. Of the 195 countries in the world, only four are still using miles and inches, Liberia, Myanmar (Burma), and the United States of America. The United Kingdom is the fourth, officially metric but in practice imperial measures still dominate; *see also, Kilometer.*

**MILLENNIAL TEACHERS** Veteran teachers can entertain these young colleagues with history lessons about teaching with chalk, writing on blackboards and overhead projectors, using print encyclopedias, and teaching attentive and obedient students; *see also, Uphill Both Ways.*

**MISHAPS OF CLASSROOM TECHNOLOGY** Not much can go wrong when a teacher uses books. As long as there are enough to go around and they are not badly damaged, books are consistent. Not so with technology. The more bells and whistles the techno-device has (and the salesperson was sure to tell the principal every single one of them, useful or not), the more there is that can break down. Well-planned lessons dependent on using the latest and greatest technology can go awry rather quickly if there is a software glitch, a hardware malfunction or, heaven forbid, a power failure. Sometimes, the boring old-fashioned textbook is the best choice, not only for its consistency but its novelty. Several students may wonder what it is that they are holding; *see also, Improvisation, Textbook.*

**MONKS OF THE DIGITAL AGE** There are a number of similarities between the monks of the middle ages and the super technophiles of the contemporary era. Middle-ages monks were one of the few people who could read, thus making their control of information-flow pretty solid.

This brings to mind the software designers and network providers of today who have become the new controllers. When the technocrats have that level of hegemony, there is little motivation to broaden the knowledge or skill level of others. Power shared is power diminished. Could the education system take on the challenge of developing the tech literacy level of the masses and be as successful as it once did with reading and writing? Will the monks of the digital age do every-thing they can to prevent it? *see also, Idea Thread Mapper.*

**MONOLOGUE** Here follows an interesting question that connects a principal's rambling explanation at a faculty meeting with two theatrical terms. Is such rambling a monologue? (defined by the person yakking while the others can hear though may not listen). Or is the pontification more of a soliloquy (in which the person yaks and the others cannot hear), due to quality shortcomings of either the presenter or the material; *see also, Laser Eyes, Quibble, White Noise (b).*

# N

**NAME-DROPPER** Those people adept at edubabble terms realize that such fluff can only go so far. When glazed eyes and a vacant expression is the response to the latest terms being spouted, the truly adept make a sudden switch to name-dropping. Most listeners are more interested in people-gossip than edubabble-lingo, especially when impropriety may be involved. As captivating as edubabble is, it cannot match the attention span commanded by a possible scandal involving those higher up the political or educational food chain; *see also, Term-Dropper.*

**NAMES AND TITLES - SCIENCE** A nifty title can add a lot of grandeur to a name and sticking the word science to the end must provide a measure of *gravitas*. Initially there was the Social Sciences, followed by Animal Science and Managerial Science. In the 1980s Computer Science was added. Now there is Custodial Science, Consumer Science, and Learning Science.

What's next? Borrowing from contemporary politicians and "news" outlets, does the study of English become Fictional Science and Drama renamed, Theatrical Science? *see also, FACSE, Journal of Learning Sciences, Library Science, Management Science.*

**NAMES - STUDENTS** Any veteran teacher has a good idea about the rise and fall of popular baby names. Popular girls' names in the 1980s and 90s were Jessica, Ashley, and Amanda. By 2000-2010 Sarah, Emily, and Chloe were top five in popularity. For boys, the 1980-90's period featured Christopher, Matthew, and Michael. In the next decade it was Joshua, Jack, and Thomas. Once popular names such as Claudine, Nanette, Horatio, and Archie have not yet made a comeback. However, with Prince Harry and Megan Markle naming their first child Archie, there may be an upsurge in that moniker. On the off chance any second child of the royal couple is a girl named Veronica, questions may be asked about the couple's choice of literature being too closely linked to Archie comic books.

Of course, some names are never popular. It would be a rarity for a teacher to instruct a student named Judas, Medusa, or Adolf.

**NAMING OF POSITIONS** When everyone expects a promotion after a period of time, imagination is required to devise a ranking system with commensurate pay. The military has devised an impressive system of "classes" as in Private First Class. There is also deft use of adjectives such as Lieutenant General and Major General. At times the adjective seems nonsensical. Is a Rear Admiral higher or lower on the food chain than a "Frontal" Admiral? To make matters even more interesting, stars are used, as in Five-Star General.

The education system is far behind such categorical division. There are only rare locales where a position such as "Teacher First Class" is used. Seniority may drive up pay but the title of teacher remains the same.

However, once a person climbs higher up the hierarchal food chain, the system begins to demonstrate some bureaucratic creativity when assigning positional rank. There are Vice-Principals, Assistant Principals, and Deputy Principals. There are Assistant Superintendents, Area Superintendents, and Deputy Superintendents. Most teachers don't know or care about the nuances involved in each title but the people in those positions do. They know where they stand in the food chain and are well aware of who they can eat and who can eat them; *see also, Assistant Principal, Quartermaster.*

**NANTUCKET** This island off the coast of Massachusetts is an extremely popular last word of the first line in teen-authored Limericks. This leaves an open spot for a relatively easy rhyme for the last word of the second line; *see also, F-Bomb, Limerick, Obscenity and Profanity.*

**NATURAL HIGH** Only a teacher knows the feeling of trying to explain a concept in several different ways only to receive looks of puzzlement or frustration from the student. Then, in one ecstatic moment, the student's eyes light up as if jolted by electricity. A wide grin creases the face. Understanding has been achieved. For the teacher, the natural high that results from moments such as this makes the horrors of the education bureaucracy melt away.

**NEGATIVE NOBILITY (THE)** Fortunately, only few parents suffer from this affliction that is close to an addiction. When infected, the symptoms are unpleasant and a cure elusive. These parents complain about everything from the salient to the trivial. They do so at decibel levels approaching that of a rock band as well as faint whispers in the school parking lot. They use old-fashioned methods such as letters to the editor of the local newspaper and contemporary social media such as twitter. For all these reasons, they stand out, not noble in behavior but as a member of a special caste, complaint addicts. Referring to them publicly as the Lord or Lady of the Complaint Manor is not a good idea; *see also, Time Vampires.*

**NEUROSCIENCE** Education professors and researchers so want education to be seen as a true scientific discipline. A workable definition of neuroscience, borrowed from *Medical News Today* states that, "Neuroscientists focus on the brain and its impact on behavior and cognitive functions." It would be logical to assume that the education researchers would be involved in what was described as an "Interdisciplinary" approach.

Alas, this is not the case. In that *Medical News Today* website, mathematics, linguistics, engineering, computer science, chemistry, philosophy, psychology, and medicine are listed as connected disciplines. What happened to education?

Perhaps it is only that definition that ignores the work of education researchers. That too, is not the case. Wikipedia has a similar list of disciplines linked to neuroscience as does the Georgetown Department of Neuroscience. Education is not mentioned in any of these sites, making it abundantly clear what people in other disciplines think of the scientific research in the education field; *see also, Evidence-Based Practice, Journal of Learning Sciences, Oligarchs in Education (d).*

**NEW ART FORM** It is always difficult to offer what high school students believe to be relevant curriculum. Economic needs change quickly. So do cultural trends. Some "needs" are nothing more than a media-driven fad, soon to whither on the proverbial vine. Some programs require considerable injections of capital and there is always the danger of making an error and being left with a white elephant of material and equipment.

The new "vibe" of linking Art to technology, though potentially expensive, has considerable promise. Firstly, such connections are hardly new and both Art and Technology have demonstrated staying power over decades if not centuries (though in various guises). Society is clearly visually and technologically oriented. This an opportunity for a marriage between the stereotypical "free-form" artists and the concrete-sequential techies. Opposites do attract, even in marriages of convenience; *see also, Hotbeds of Dissent, Mickey Mouse, Website Project.*

**NEW SCHOOL NERVES** It is natural for a teacher to be anxious on the first day in a new school. The students and teacher-colleagues will be unfamiliar. Perhaps the principal did not seem all that anxious to have you on the faculty. Calming those nerves with three jumbo cups of heavy-duty java can transform jitters into an exuberant caffeine high. Truly buzzed, the newbie will explode with vigor and enthusiasm. Students, colleagues, and administrators will be suitably impressed; *see also, Jolt of Caffeine.*

**NEWSCHOOLS VENTURE FUND** This US non-profit philanthropy promotes education entrepreneurs who, according to their website, invested nearly 260 million in nearly 470 schools in eighteen years. Many of their donors are extremely wealthy people. Their website states, "NewSchools founders believed that education entrepreneurs could . . . bring about much-needed change in public education if they had access to both early-stage capital and strategic, hands-on support to start and grow their organizations." At a later point in the website, "Our work to invest in schools initially focused on driving accountability and enabling choice for families."

Interestingly, attendance at the annual summit (not conference) is by invitation only; *see also, Conferences, Edupreneurs, Oligarchs in Education.*

**NEWSLETTERS** If a teacher is having difficulty with insomnia, a free non-prescription remedy may be at hand. Try reading your school's newsletter late at night. It is propaganda to be sure, especially if one defines propaganda as providing only one side of a story. There will be no mention of anything that could even remotely be construed as negative about the school. In addition, the information is presented in mind-numbing sameness, making boring the most favorable description available. You may find yourself waking in the morning refreshed after a wonderful night's sleep with the newsletter laying by your side. To continue with happy slumber simply print another school's newsletter. They're all identical in layout, verbiage, and quality; *see also, Principal's Message.*

**NEW TEXTING ABBREVIATIONS** Even most elderly educators are familiar with at least some text abbreviations such as BFF (best friends forever), LMK, (let me know), and WTF (what the f . . .). There will be times when a teacher will wish to engage in surreptitious texting and some helpful abbreviations could be:

a) DD – Damn duty; at recess, lunch, or after school;

b) PY – Principal yakking (at a faculty meeting);

c) WGT – Wine guzzling time (after work, presumably);

d) GT – Grading tonight, or Gin and Tonic, or both simultaneously;

e) WK – Whiny kid (anytime).

**NORMS** Once a popular and widely used term, norms were based on "normal" academic progress, behavior, or skill level. What constitutes "normal" in contemporary society is certainly debatable. What is a "normal" family? What does "normal" sexual development look like? Is "normal" teen behavior the same for the privileged student compared to the one living in abject poverty? Measuring students against academic, behavioral, or social norms when "normal" really does not exist seems abnormally out-of-date; *see also, Unschoolers.*

**NOTICES - BULLETIN BOARD** Few read these that are posted in the teachers' lounge, yet no one takes them down. The thumbtack acts as glue, keeping the notice pinned to the board long after whatever message was being advertised is valid. By mid-year there is no room left on any of the boards. Still, no one has the time, or guts, to take anything down. Notices get piled on top of older ones, sometimes three-thick. At the end of the school year some brave soul will take them down, usually exclaiming something like, "Oh look, I didn't know Julie was selling her car," or, "If I had known about that reading conference, I might have gone."

**NUMBER NUMBNESS** "A billion here, a billion there, pretty soon you're into real money." 1960s Illinois senator Everett Dirksen was often credited with that phrase. Though it appears that he was misquoted, the statement does indicate the difficulty in coming to grips with extremely large numbers. Scientists and mathematicians will state that the use of logarithms help, but few lay people understand these. When teaching basic paleontology or geology, hundreds of millions of years ago is not likely to make much sense to a fifteen-year-old student who thinks a long time ago was being enrolled in the seventh grade. Similarly, the distances involved in space travel are unfathomable when the youth thinks a three-hundred-mile car ride equals excruciatingly long boredom.

# O

**OBSCENITY AND PROFANITY** A teacher can always learn something from the students, including new vocabulary. Not only can their students can come up with all manner of previously little-known profanity, they display creativity in varying the usage of the more common obscenities to keep their speech fresh and alive; *see also, F-Bomb, Language Acquisition-Teachers, Limerick, Nantucket, White Noise (d)*.

**OLIGARCHS IN EDUCATION** The most common use of the term oligarchs refers to the powerful in Russia, a small cadre of extremely wealthy individuals who exert control and influence over the government. Oligarchs exist in the West as well, their activity perhaps not as dramatic yet still influential. They can be found in business, the military, and in government. Even education has a semblance of oligarchic influence. Though unusually broad in number, these people have impact in determining the direction of major shifts and trends in schools. These education oligarchs share particular characteristics, some of which are:

a) Holding doctoral degrees in Education with impressive titles, rather than the "inconsequential" Bachelors degrees held by the majority of teachers; *see also, Doctorate Degrees in Education;*

b) Never having taught in a public-school classroom;

c) Writing articles in academic journals of education that no one except fellow oligarchs and their wannabes-in-training read, let alone understand; *see also, Journal of Learning Sciences;*

d) Working in a university with the primary goal of moving the status of education as a research discipline up from the bottom of the academic pile; *see also, Neuroscience;*

e) Convincing government officials that their advice about schools, no matter how impractical, should be foisted onto teachers;

f) Lamenting the ineptness of the system when their ideas fail miserably when put into practice;

*see also, NewSchools Venture Fund.*


**ONE-DAY BREAK** One day passes by another without much fanfare during the summer holidays. Not so during the school year. A Monday or Friday off due to a national holiday is a major treat. Weather-related school cancelations can provide welcome relief as long as shoveling snow or hurricane prevention work does not take up the entire day. The scarcity of these one-day breaks makes them all the more valuable. This lends credence to the classical economist view about pricing. When demand far outstrips supply, the value of whatever is being supplied is very high.

**ONE HUNDRED THIRTY-TWO** This seemingly innocuous number means a great deal to some people. While many educators do not hold much store in the validity of IQ tests, those who are members of Mensa might. Their IQ score would be the determining factor in gaining entrance to the group since a candidate must score in the 98th percentile on a validated IQ test. The minimum standard is a score of 132 on the Stanford-Binet or 148 on the Cattell Culture Fair Intelligence Test. For practice a person can try a few questions on the internet. Presumably, a teacher-sponsor of a Mensa for Teens group in a school would qualify as a member or risk potential credibility issues; *see also, Intelligence Testing-Masses, Teacher of the Gifted.*

**ONE KID LIKE YOU** One of the interesting side aspects of years in the classroom is the discovery that a few students will remind you of your own adolescence. Perhaps it is the student's love of a sport, a musical instrument, singing, or a particular sense of humor that brings a wry smile.

The connection may deepen however. In a long teaching career, there is a probability that there will be a student who not only has similar likes and dislikes but bears a striking resemblance to the teacher when the adult was an adolescent. This may be a pleasant, though slightly unnerving, experience for the teacher, working with a younger version of yourself. However, it may not be as pleasant for those students who have also noticed the similarity. Anxious thoughts may enter the student's mind, such as, "Holy crap, is that what I'm gonna look like in twenty years?"

**OPTICAL MARK READER** Multiple choice tests may be out of vogue in contemporary public education circles but it is likely that a number of teachers continue to use this type of assessment. The Optical Mark Reader and accompanying bubble sheets make grading tests a veritable breeze. If the school still has a reader, it is best stored in an area less frequented by edubabbler colleagues. Some bandwagoners may wish to have the device banished from the building; *see also, Unit of Study.*

**ORACY** Good edubabble can often be as easy as using an obscure term to describe a relatively common activity. If a person states that she or he is working on developing oracy with the students, it simply means developing the ability to communicate clearly using speech; *see also, Edubabble–Characteristics (c), Obscenity and Profanity.*

**ORAL FIXATION** Just because toddlers like to put everything in their mouths does not mean that the tendency has fully dissipated when the students reach high school. Teachers must be aware of students munching on a rarely found ruler or the end of an even more rare pencil. A teen spending an hour gleefully licking a glue stick in Art class may display some interesting side effects, prompting a visit from the school nurse, the principal, or both. At the end of the day the teacher may wish to engage in a similar type of oral fixation involving fermented grape juice; *see also, Homemade Wine.*

**ORCHESTRAL CLASS** Instruments played poorly do not make for pleasant listening. String instruments are particularly noteworthy on the horrific sound meter with violins and violas leading the pack on the screeching scale. Any teacher assigned to the Beginner Orchestra class will require a monthly hearing test, lest the brain, in a desperate attempt at self-preservation, may have ordered the ears to shut down; *see also, Guitar Class.*

**OSTRACIZED** As a general rule, teaching is a supportive profession. Despite this, there are certain behaviors or position statements that may lead to a teacher being ostracized, especially by particular groups of colleagues. Examples are:

a) The teacher who questions the impact sports teams have on the school's budget and culture; *see also, Losing Seasons;*

b) The Psychology teacher who teaches the students about phallic symbols and sends them on a quest for examples throughout the school; *see also, Phallic Symbol;*

c) Any teacher who believes the school's Parent Council should have more authority over programs and instructional delivery;

d) Any teacher who believes that the salary is reasonable.

# P

**PARKING LOT - STUDENT** In some affluent schools it is easy to discern the vehicle parking area for teachers from that for the students. The teacher parking lot is filled with "vintage" Chevrolets, Dodge mini-vans, and mainstream SUVs built by Honda or Toyota. The student area is filled with freshly washed BMW's, Volvos, and Cadillac SUV's, with a Lexus or two thrown in for good measure.

**PARKINSON'S LAW** This "law" of employment states that work expands to fill the space provided, meaning some people who don't have enough to do will find a way to look busy. Teachers in schools do not need to fill in empty time, there is more than enough for them to do in a day. Education researchers, education professors, and more than a few education bureaucrats, do. One manner of filling in the time is inventing and debating the merits of new edubabble and then foisting the accompanying "innovation" onto teachers; *see also, Dinky Districts, Pedagogy (2)*.

**PEDAGOGY** There is not enough space in this glossary to present the varying definitions of pedagogy, so a relatively simple definition will suffice; "The theory and practice of educating." As for the connection to edubabble, there are two interesting questions regarding pedagogy.

1. Does teaching lean more toward an art or a science? This is a topic of interest to teachers and it is likely that most would believe that teaching falls more on the art side of the fence, despite the attempts of education researchers and some practitioners to push the scientific aspect of teaching; *see also, FACSE, Journal of Learning Sciences, Library Science, Names and Titles-Science, Neuroscience*.

2. How does pedagogy differ from heutagogy? It is impossible to believe that a busy teacher would care about this topic, leaving such distinction to those with much more time on their hands; *see also, Heutagogy, Parkinson's Law*.

**PENMANSHIP** *see Writing-Cursive*.

**PERIODIC TABLE OF THE ELEMENTS** Introducing the schema of the periodic table is a challenging task for a science teacher. Firstly, unlike most tables, it is irregular in shape. Secondly, again unlike most tables, it has "mini-tables" tucked inside. The seven period rows, the columnar groups, and the rectangular blocks, all indicate different chemical properties. While this latter point is beyond the ken of those students being introduced to the table, at least the abbreviations make sense. It is easily understood that H stands for Hydrogen, C for Carbon, and even the "weird ones" like #107 Bohrium, has an easily understood Bh as an abbreviation.

Unfortunately, not all in science is at it seems. Eventually a student is going to ask why Fe is the abbreviation for Iron, Na for Sodium, and Hg for Mercury. This makes one of the few occasions where a titch of Latin is useful; *see also, Klingon, Krypton.*

**PETER PRINCIPLE** Rising to the level of one's incompetence is the main thrust of this famous 1969 book. Laurence Peters noted that competent people were promoted based on outputs until they reached a level in the hierarchy at which they were incompetent. Instead of being terminated, Peter noticed that the incompetent employee was more often evaluated on inputs such as having a positive attitude, rather than the outputs on which they were previously judged. Only extremely incompetent employees were terminated from employment.

Before educators begin to chuckle about the follies of hierarchies in business organizations and the military, it should be noted that Peters began his career as a public-school teacher in Vancouver, BC and was an education professor in California when he wrote the book.

**PHALLIC SYMBOL** When teaching Psychology there are many aspects of Freudian assertions that should be avoided. This is one of them. Should a teacher provide a stimulating lesson about phallic symbols, a Frankenstein-like monster could be created that cannot be controlled. Members of the class may soon be zipping about the school, seeing phallic symbols in all manner of places, including the attire of many teachers. This activity has the potential for some embarrassing moments. The teacher who set this train in motion can expect to be shunned in the teachers' lounge for at least a week; *see also, Ostracized (c)*.

**PHONEMIC AWARENESS** Phonemic awareness is the student's ability to identify and combine phonemes in words by segmenting and blending. This skill is a good predictor of later reading ability. Most high school teachers, even those with English degrees, do not know much about phonemic awareness and certainly not how to develop it in students. Teaching strategies to improve reading such as, "Read it louder," or "Skip a word or two and get the general gist," are not much help in providing assistance to the struggling teenage reader.

**PHOTOCOPIER** The school may have networked computers and high-speed internet on optic cabling. There may be smart-boards and high-resolution projection screens. Despite the high-tech gadgetry, the photocopier remains the most valued piece of equipment in the school, tied for first place with the coffee maker and just ahead of the dishwasher.

**PISA** Federal politicians in the United States often state that the country is, "The richest in the world," or that it boasts, "The mightiest military." Leaders like to note America's rank in any category when it is in the top three on the planet. But politicians do not feel inclined to talk about their jurisdiction being consistently rated as "middling", so few US leaders talk publicly about the results from the Programme for International Student Assessment. This program has been conducted around the world every three years since 2000. It assesses fifteen-year-old students in Mathematics, Science, and Reading. In 2018, 600,000 students were assessed in seventy-nine jurisdictions.

The 2018 assessment results were released in December of 2019. The rankings (out of seventy-nine) for the United States and Canada were:

a) in Reading the United States was ranked 13th, Canada 6th;

b) in Mathematics the United States was ranked 37th, Canada 12th;

c) in Science the United States was ranked 18th, Canada 8th.

Whatever one believes about this type of assessment (and of course caution should be exercised when analyzing the results), the performance level of the United States has been relatively consistent over time (as has Canada's). This educational ranking does not come close to matching the level of US economic or military might. This may provide some hint as to broad national priorities.

In the December 2019 figures, student scores in a Chinese region were the top ranking in all three categories. Singapore was second in all three categories and Macau third. The top-ranked non-Asian country was Estonia which was 5th in Reading, 8th in Mathematics, and 4th in Science; *see also, Ranking of Schools.*

**PLAGIARISM** Today's students live in a veritable candy store of information. Snatching a ready-made essay on whatever topic is needed is similar to previous generations purchasing bubble gum at the local convenience store. Just as there is a manufacturer's suggested retail price for goods (MSRP), essays can come with a something akin to a SRLG (suppliers recommended letter grade). The customer can pay a high fee for an A-grade paper or get the cheaper C-grade version. Never has plagiarism been so easy and so commercial.

**POPCORN** If for some bizarre reason a teacher wishes to go out of their way to annoy the custodial staff, begin selling popcorn every day at lunch. Students will find it hard to resist dumping handfuls of the kernels on other student's heads. Spilling the light airy stuff is inevitable and sweeping it up is difficult. Beware, the custodian will not likely take this sitting down. Payback may be in order. Keys to the filing cabinet may go "missing." The shelves in the classroom may get a little dusty. There may not be any student replacement desks in the storage room. While the team or club that the teacher sponsors may be making a significant amount of money from popcorn sales (the margins are ridiculously high), do the repercussions really make it worthwhile?

Avoid offering a cut of the profits to the custodian who likely has far higher ethical standards than many politicians or tycoon CEOs. The offer will be rebuked and seen as an insult, thus driving a deeper wedge between teacher and custodian; *see also, Ethical Standards.*

**POT** *see Gateway Drug, Weed, Zoned Out.*

**PRACTICUM** It is necessary to have student teachers obtain experience in a classroom prior to their certification. When a student-teacher is on a practicum, the sponsoring teacher is the person doing most of the supervision by providing advice and guidance and writing reports. The university supervisor is often a distant second in influencing the student-teacher, particularly during lengthy practicums. Of course, the student is paying a tuition fee that is gobbled up whole by the university. Shouldn't the person and the organization doing most of the work—the supervising teacher and the school, receive at least a portion of that tuition?

**PRINCIPAL'S MESSAGE** Principals must love writing these fables. They are found on websites, in yearbooks, and in the programs for theatrical performances and athletic tournaments. They often adorn a graduation ceremony pamphlet. There is little variation from event to event and principal to principal. There is certainly nothing creative or illuminating from a literary point of view. The single most notable feature of these messages is that no one reads them. This leaves a singular question worthy of at least some attention. If these messages all sound the same, and nobody reads them, why do principals spend time writing them? *see also, Newsletters.*

**PUBLIC ADDRESS SYSTEM** As with politicians, many principals never met a microphone they did not like. Parental gatherings such as music concerts provide opportunities, but over the course of a school-year they are relatively few in number. Not so with the PA system. Every day brings fresh opportunities, the microphone close at hand and the connected speakers on the wall of every classroom. The principal can yak each day, sometimes more than a few times. Perhaps some principals had dreams of being a disc jockey or are simply in love with their dulcet tones; *see also, Droning.*

# Q

**QUALIFICATIONS FOR ADMINISTRATORS** While the usual path to become a principal or superintendent in North America is to have had experience as a teacher, it is not always the case. In the United States qualification standards are set by districts and/or states. A greater number of states are enacting legislation to make it easier for people with little or no teaching experience to be placed as superintendents and even in some cases, principals. The basis for such a policy is that a superintendent is more likely to spend a great deal of time on policy, labor negotiations, public relations, and finance, all matters that require a different background from that of most teachers.

This seems like a logical argument until it is noted that the same may be said of the type of work performed by colonels and generals as distinct from soldiers. Despite this, it would be difficult to imagine a high-ranking officer never having experience as a soldier.

Perhaps the education system is paving the way for administration to be regarded as a separate profession, disconnected experientially from those working in the system being administered. If former generals can be superintendents, can ex-principals be colonels?

**QUARTERBACK** Football can mirror life—victory and defeat, long runs and hard knocks, deft dekes, and ill-timed fumbles. Ex-jock or not, there are more than a few principals who would love to be the quarterback of the school for the following reasons:

a) Since the quarterback controls the ball at the start of every play, he (and it is almost always a male) must decide whether to proceed with the agreed-upon play or improvise. Most principals would love that level of control;

b) When the team is in the huddle, the quarterback calls the play. It is rare for any team members to question the decision. There is no attempt to "build consensus" and "get everyone on board." The members are expected to follow the quarterback's call, quickly and without debate. What principal would not appreciate that power and have more faculty meetings resembling football huddles? *see also, Weed.*

**QUARTERMASTER** In the army the quartermaster holds a powerful position, responsible for supervising stores and distributing supplies and provisions. In schools this person is called the Head Secretary, or the

Administrative Assistant, or Assistant to the Principal, or more colloquially, the Office Head Honcho.

**QUESTIONS IN INTERVIEWS - STRATEGY ONE** During a job interview it is likely that there will be at least one question on a topic in which the interviewee is totally clueless. Some candidates will attempt to fire off some edubabble. This is a risky proposition since the principal may be more proficient at sloganeering jargon than you. Another strategy is to prattle on and on, hopeful that if enough words come out a few will hit the mark. This spewing of fluff only results in an effective display of your ignorance.

A good strategy when faced with the "I don't have a clue" situation is to skirt the issue and get on to the next question as quickly as possible. Answers such as, "I've always wanted an opportunity to know more about that," or, "I admit that is not my area of expertise though one of my strengths is that I'm a quick learner," are solid responses. If you have to resort to this type of answer more than three times in a thirty-minute interview, there is a good chance you will not be the successful candidate; *see also, Term-Dropper.*

**QUESTIONS IN INTERVIEWS - STRATEGY TWO** When responding to questions in a job interview it is always best to accentuate the positive and skirt a direct answer so as to come across in the best light possible. This is not natural for many teachers who, unlike politicians, are not normally adept at self-promoting spin. A teacher interviewee may need some help and the following are examples of possible answers to the question, "What are some of the things you would like to improve on at work?"

a) "I spend too much time at school and need to achieve a better work-life balance";

b) "I spend too much time with the kids at lunch and coaching after school so I'm not in the teachers' lounge to connect with my colleagues as much as I should be";

c) "I need to realize that at the beginning of the year, reading each student's file and having lengthy discussions with the parent does not always give me the entire picture of the student";

d) "I need to cease responding to online parental questions and concerns after 9:00 pm";

e) "I must reduce the amount of personal money I am spending on classroom supplies. That will make my spouse happy";

f) "I need to attend more professional development sessions. I find that two conferences per year plus the monthly district workshops are not enough to keep me current."

**QUEUE** This term is more widely used in the United Kingdom and sounds much less militaristic than the favored North American term, "line-up." The latter term also has an unfavorable connection to a police station. When a teacher picks a student out of a line-up, the action has connotations linked to a witness identifying a criminal and having the police haul the offender away to a nearby jail cell.

**QUIBBLE** Since one purpose of edubabble is to obfuscate, disagreements about the meaning of certain terms or phrases is to be expected. Teachers are generally polite people and the intellectual stakes in any edubabble debate are abysmally low. Therefore, rather than heated arguments, one can expect a certain amount of quibbling every now and then. Some examples are:

1. "I don't know if the library operation truly meets the standard of a Learning Commons"; *see also, Learning Commons;*
2. "I don't know if that activity should be regarded as kinesthetic or tactile learning"; *see also, Kinesthetic/ Tactile Learning;*
3. "Perhaps the name for our gifted program should be altered to the Gifted and Talented program"; *see also, G and T, Teacher of the Gifted;*
4. "Should we employ convergent or divergent thinking to come to a solution about where and when to hold the staff party?" *see also, Meta-Cognition, Thinking;*
5. "At the next workshop I want to clarify whether the new curriculum is process or product based"; *see also, Curriculum Process/Product.*

**QUICK WRITE** This teaching technique is a version of "writing on demand" and it is not surprising that many students fail to fire up the creative juices when subjected to their teacher's love of the timed forced write.

**QUID PRO QUO** For a few high school teachers assigned to classes filled with disengaged and rebellious youth, there may be a need for a semi-formal arrangement with particularly recalcitrant teens. An understanding from the teacher to student such as, "I will get off your case if you simply show up for class and do at least a bit of work without bothering others," may work.

Any situation that entices a principal to approach a teacher with a similar type of "deal" has likely moved beyond what most people would construe to be a professional relationship; *see also, Kickbacks, Letters of Reference (1)*.

**QUINOA** North Americans have "discovered" this "new" food, though it has been popular in what is now Peru and Bolivia for thousands of years. It has taken on a faddish appeal. Anything that nutritious, that popular, that fast, is bound to get some people worked up about instituting it as a lunch time staple in schools. Hot dogs, hamburgers, and pizza are hardly strong competitors in any proper-nutrition contest. Quinoa is also gluten-free, but so many foods are now advertised as such there may be a time when packaging states "Gluten Included" just to stand out from the crowd; *see also, Culinary Correctness, Kale, Vending Machines*.

**QUIZ - SNAP** The students who dislike these evaluative tools usually fall into one of the following major categories:

a) Those who are comfortable with a routinized classroom and become anxious at the change of activity;

b) Those who like to be prepared and become nervy at not being able to study beforehand;

c) Those who are unable to duplicate their usual feat of obtaining many of the test questions beforehand from students in the same course with a class that meets prior to theirs;

d) Those who are unable to miss the quiz by skipping class.

# R

**RAP MUSIC** In the 1960s it would be very unusual for a high school music teacher to have a rhythm and blues stage band or vocal group. Many music teachers of the day thought such music was not to be promoted in school. Today, whether it be nostalgia, a shift in the attitudes of music teachers, an attempt to recruit new students to the program, or to retain the ones already enrolled, R&B groups can be found as a component in many music programs.

Few contemporary music directors are willing to travel down the road of introducing rap or hip-hop to the program. Many likely feel much the same way about that music as the teachers did in the 1960s about R&B. Does this similarity portend a future? Fifty years from now will rap and hip-hop be a relatively common component of a high school music program? One shudders to think so; *see also, Jesus Christ Superstar.*

**RATING OF SCHOOLS** Society is so obsessed with rankings it seems like a national pastime. There is a top ten, or top fifty or top whatever number, for the best baseball players, the dumbest criminals, the biggest grossing movie, the closest election results, the top sports mishaps, the most influential record albums, and on, and on, and on.

It is not surprising that ranking schools by test results has become common. It does not seem to matter whether the measurement being used is valid or if there are significant extraneous factors influencing the result. A ranking has the illusion of clear information. There are winners (assuming the rating is from best to worst), and there are losers. Many people want to identify with the former and pity or even ridicule the latter; *see also, Abstinence, PISA.*

**RECRUITING** It is nice to feel wanted. Especially when you are either a skilled, coordinated teen basketball center six inches taller than your opponents, or a large, muscled, small-necked adolescent linebacker with an on-field personality that rivals Darth Vader. It seems natural that such "stars" would be recruited by certain high schools despite rules in place barring such activity in many jurisdictions.

If that is so, why does it seem strange for there to be recruiting for a talented actor with a captivating stage presence, a gifted teenage concert pianist, or a young sculptor who is well-regarded in the local visual arts community? *see also, Losing Seasons.*

**RED SCHOOL HOUSE** One of the goals of this glossary is to enable teachers to spout off inane trivia and become a school version of the Cliff Clavin character on the old sitcom *Cheers*. A colleague may wonder why old schoolhouses and barns were painted red. Most teachers would not know the answer. But thanks to reading the *High School Edubabble*, you do.

In the 1800s, iron oxide was a readily available pigment to be used in paint that was excellent as a wood preservative. Iron oxide is most often a reddish color, similar to rust. A little skilled mixing of the pigment and paint made for a more pleasing red. The most common use of iron oxide today is as a coloring agent in the cosmetics industry.

If no colleague ever asks the question, you may have to initiate the conversation. Do not be too obvious. Making a comment on the current drab paint covering the school's exterior may eventually lead nicely into the origins of schoolhouse red; *see also, Know-It-All Colleague, Yellow School Bus.*

**REPORTING OUT AT WORKSHOPS** Group discussions are the norm at teacher workshops. And when these take place there is usually a reporting-out responsibility tasked to each group. Unless you won the prize for "most eager" at the local Toastmasters workshop, or are rehearsing for a moonlighting stand-up comedy routine, this is a responsibility that is best to avoid. You may be in the group with the most nonsensical ideas and find yourself announcing a position so different from all others that your report will be followed by hearty laughter or stunned silence, neither of which will give you positive vibes. Some of the pitfalls that may befall the "reporter" are:

a) Your group may have been totally off task, yakking about sports, or fashion, or politics. Thus, you will be left with having to talk about nothing or begin to spout a great deal of edubabble, which is really much the same thing;

b) Though your group may have stayed on task, the group reporting before yours might state exactly what you were about to say. You are left with providing a report that sounds akin to, "Our group came to the same conclusions those guys did," which seems more than just a tad lame;

c) Your group may have included a cadre of disaffected grousing grumblers who are bent on subverting the purpose of the workshop with ill-advised sarcasm. As the official reporter, you will appear rebellious, rude, impertinent, boorish, or all of the above.

**RESEARCH IN EDUCATION** *see Action Research, Doctorate Degrees in Education, Evidence-Based Practice, Neuroscience, Parkinson's Law.*

**RESTROOM GRAFFITI** There are some behaviors from university days that should not be duplicated when a person begins a teaching career. One example is attending mid-week alcohol-fueled parties. Another is writing graffiti on restroom walls. Admittedly the graffiti in university restrooms is an intellectual step or two above that penned on bus station stalls, but clever quips and scathing satire is best left off the school's restrooms. Should one feel the need for some sagacious satire to spice up a bathroom break, purchase copies of *Edubabble* and *High School Edubabble* and leave them in the teacher restroom for all to enjoy.

**RHYTHM** Every teacher finds a word that many students find difficult to spell year-after-year. The teacher also struggles to spell it correctly. Rhythym . . . rhthym . . . rhythm is one such example.

**RIFLE PROGRAMS** According to a 2018 article in *The Guardian* newspaper there are over 2,000 high school rifle programs in the United States. The statistic speaks for itself.

**RIVALRY – SIBLING** *see Bad Egg of the Family.*

**ROBOTICS COMPETITIONS** Eventually the major robotics competitions may become similar to state or province-wide athletic tournaments with scouts scattered throughout the crowd. Universities are always looking for talent, especially in areas that make them money, sports and corporate donations being two particularly deep money pits. Corporations wishing to get an upper-hand in automation and thus throw even more humans out of work, may pick up some excellent robotics prospects. They can season these youngsters in a small subsidiary, the corporate equivalent of the minor leagues in sports. If the prospect does not realize full potential, perhaps a trade to another firm for future draft picks is always possible; *see also, University Admissions.*

**ROMANTIC POETS** Many adolescents are drawn to rebels who lead interesting lives and pass away while young. Though poetry is not currently popular, a review of the lives of some of the notable Romantic Poets of the 19th century may stimulate teen interest and spice up an English lesson or two. Percy Bysshe Shelley, Lord Byron, and John Keats led angst-driven lives, railed against the standards of the day, and passed away while young men. Some additional notes of interest that several contemporary teens may regard as "cool" are:

a) Shelly advocated non-violent resistance, and his writing had an impact on Gandhi and Martin Luther King. He was expelled from school. His wife, Mary, wrote Frankenstein and he hung out with Lord Byron; *see also, Expulsion from School (1);*

b) Byron was a celebrity of Kardashian proportions, perhaps even more so due to his aristocratic background. With a flamboyant persona, he led a life of excess, eventually joining the revolutionary movement for Greek independence; *see also, Anti-Educators (c);*

c) Despite passing his surgeon's exams, Keats chose to be a poet even though he was not well-received as a writer. The generally conservative reviewers of the day found his work vulgar;

*see also, Hotbeds of Dissent.*

# S

**SCOPES, JOHN** On occasion a teacher "takes one for the team." Little known even among science teachers, Mr. Scopes nonetheless helped pave the way for changes to the way scientific knowledge, specifically evolution, was taught in public schools. The Scopes "Monkey Trial" in the mid 1920s involved Mr. Scopes being accused of teaching evolution to the students in his science class. The entire episode is fascinating for much more than the impact on the future of science education.

1. The American Civil Liberties Association was looking for a "volunteer" to admit to teaching evolution so there would be an opportunity to challenge the law in court. John Scopes, somewhat reluctantly, agreed.
2. Though teaching evolution was against the law in Tennessee, teachers were obligated to follow the textbook, which contained a chapter on evolution.
3. A trial could not have two bigger legal heavyweights than William Jennings Byron, a former

three-time Presidential candidate for the Democratic Party, who helped represent the State of Tennessee, and Clarence Darrow who was a leader on the team for the defense.

4. Mr. Scopes was found guilty and fined $100.00 (about $1,400.00 in 2020 dollars) but the award was overturned on a technicality.

5. Mr. Scopes later attended a Masters Program in Geology since he was barred from teaching in Tennessee. He was hounded by a media circus for years to come.

6. The entire affair was made into a movie, *Inherit the Wind* in 1960. The film reportedly takes liberty with the facts and the portrayal of William Jennings Byron is over-the-top negative.

**SCREEN ADDICTS** A blank expression, unblinking eyes, seemingly defective ears, calloused thumb tips—these are some of the characteristics of a new type of student junkie; those addicted to their screens. Unlike other junkies who have to search for their high, the screen addict usually has what he or she needs in hand. Thus, serenity and equanimity are the norm. The screen addicts do share a common behavioral bond with their junkie brethren if the fix is removed. Whining, snorting, and snarling will occur. There may even be some negative physical reactions. Teachers who intend to confiscate tech devices from these junkies should exercise caution; *see also, Fortnite, Textbook, Thumb Tapping, World Cup of Fortnite, Zoned Out.*

**SEMIVOWEL** This term is sound edubabble just as "semi-waterfront" is good realtor babble. The term sounds far more impressive than it actually is. Providing the reader with one more tool in the edubabble box, a semivowel sounds like a vowel but is not the central sound in a syllable, such as the opening of words such as yet or wet.

**SITUATED LEARNING** Sometimes it is necessary to give credit where credit is due. The following gem of fluffy, nonsensical edubabble is from IGI Global Disseminator of Knowledge, found on the internet (Driscoll 2000).

"The paradigm of situated cognition has a socio-constructivist perspective. It claims that the knowledge construction process is intricately related to the context of practice where it takes place. This theory shifts the emphasis from the individual to the socio-cultural and, in this sense, it allows us to conceptualize the teaching and learning process as a complex system of human activity. For this paradigm, learning is understood as participation in a community of practice."

This could have been stated with much less fluff, emphasizing that effective learning is enhanced by social engagement in specialized situations. Gardens as classrooms, cooperative education featuring work experience, and apprenticeship training are good examples; *see also, Journal of Learning Sciences, Oligarchs in Education (c), Visual Learning.*

**SMOKE PIT** During a real or imagined "newsworthy" event, the media bees swarm to a high school to gather intel for their reports. It is always desirable to solicit student opinion. Since the media is not usually permitted on school grounds, the swarm must find the area where students congregate off school property. Fortunately for the "journalist," most high schools have a "smoke pit" where nicotine-addicted teens are easy pickings for any reporter.

Smoke-pit students are not usually members of the Student Council, Cheerleaders, or Science Club. They often disproportionately represent a disaffected slice of the student pie. This does not prevent the media jackals from accepting the grousing from many of those in the "pit" as the unvarnished truth and reporting the information as such; *see also, Journalism, Juul, Love That Nicotine, Toxicity Pit, Under the Bus.*

**SOCCER** Easy to understand, more action than baseball, cheaper than football, less selective regarding body type than basketball, and able to be played on virtually any readily available surface unlike ice hockey, it is easy to understand why this sport is finally gaining traction in North American schools as more students are introduced to "the beautiful game"; *see also, Handball.*

**SPECIAL EDUCATION** There have been notable successes in public education over the last forty years. The drop-out rate is lower, teacher training is better, and the style of teaching is less oppressive and more student-centered. Even edubabble is more impressive with bigger words and more nifty sloganeering. Of all such improvements, none seems greater than the work in Special Education. Instead of having students fail grades and eventually drop out, or hiding them away in special schools, these students are treated with far more compassion and dignity than what was common previously. Though Special Education is renowned for its specific and prolific edubabble, that is a small price to pay for the successes the field has had; *see also, Drop Out Rate, What Were They Thinking? (d)*.

**SPIDEY SENSE** Like Spiderman, teachers have a sixth sense that is finely honed over the years. It tingles when you return to the classroom and the students are eerily quiet. It alerts you to the presence of nearby students so you refrain from profanity when talking to a colleague in the hallway after school. It warns you about the effectiveness of the upcoming school assembly when you glance at the nervous presenter; *see also, Spidey Sense Not Needed*.

**SPIDEY SENSE NOT NEEDED** In certain circumstances it is not necessary to have active spidey sense to know what is likely to happen. When a group of ninth-grade girls scamper to the restroom with the lead girl in tears, it is safe to say there has been a crisis of the heart. When a group of stern-looking teenage boys stomp across the field to the vacant lot off the school grounds, there is a likelihood that fisticuffs are uppermost in a few minds.

In a strong correlation that does not require the predictive powers of spidey sense, whenever there is unusual weather—snow in Georgia, a week of rain in Nevada, or frigid temperatures in Florida; student behavior will be equally strange. This does not portend well for the future behavior of teens since scientists predict upcoming years of freakish weather; *see also, Spidey Sense.*

**STATISTICS** The university equivalent of hell for those aspiring teachers from the humanities and arts. The reams of numbers will have little meaning or purpose when teaching in the classroom.

**STRUCTURAL FUNCTIONALISM** Education is not the only field with sloganeering and obfuscating terminology. This entry is classic sociobabble and is one of the three general groupings regarding the theories that attempt to explain the causes of juvenile delinquency (the other two broad categories being Symbolic Interactionism and Conflict Theory). Of the three, this theory is most linked to education since there is focus on institutions such as the family and school. In essence, the social processes that produce conformity to broad societal norms become strained and eventually break down. For instance, the disparity between the goals of society (monetary success), and the means to accomplish them (education), can cause friction. A subculture can develop when the underclass enters school and fails to meet middle-class expectations. Frustration grows and a subculture emerges.

Sociobabble is about as valid as edubabble, making it pretty low on the credibility scale. The brief summary above does, however, lead to thoughts about the impact on public schools if income disparity continues to widen, the middle class shrinks in number, and the values linked with it slowly dissipate.

**STUDMUFFIN** There is legitimate cause for concern if other adults use this term to describe a male teacher's persona and behavior at work. Other descriptors such as beefcake and hunk are similarly undesirable; *see also, Vixen.*

## SUPPLIES AND STORAGE - ART

1. Like colleagues in the PE department, teaching Art requires the acquisition of a significant cache of supplies and specialized equipment. Unlike PE, the Art departments in high schools usually have relatively few members and the ordering of supplies falls on fewer shoulders.

2. Like the relatively small number of colleagues teaching Cooking, those teaching Art use a great deal of consumable supplies (despite the best efforts to recycle). Unlike the culminating student activity in the Foods class, the Art supplies do not disappear into the bottomless pit of adolescent male stomachs. Very few high school students claim that their Art project is edible. If

so declared, only the truly courageous would try a nibble.

3. Like Woodwork projects, some Art pieces are large. Unlike a Woodwork shop, those designing the school provided the Art teacher with a pitiable amount of storage space.

The Art teacher will, of course, wish to display student work throughout the public areas of the school. This will not only enliven these spaces but take pressure away from having to cram the Art storage room with four times the amount of material for which it was designed to hold. Before plastering the school walls with artwork, beware of local fire regulations. There is likely an established ratio of square footage of paper to wall space that is permitted. Such stipulation may or may not be rigorously enforced.

**SWAG** This entry has several meanings—illicit loot, swagger in hip hop music, and ultra-cool lamps that hung from household ceilings in the 1970s. In one of its modern definitions swag, sometimes spelled schwag, is an acronym for, "Stuff We All Get." Examples of swag are the freebie promotional food dished out at Costco or the slippers airlines used to dispense. In education, it is the "stylish" canvas bags, sturdy binder, and various pens and notepad paper provided at education conferences. All this "free" material came at a cost. You expect to receive a few takeaways for the $1,000.00 you are forking out from your professional development fund; *see also, Conferences.*

# T

**TALKING HEADS** As new technology infiltrates the classroom, the number of teachers acting as the "sage on the stage" is gradually diminishing. A few still remain, almost exclusively in high schools. The orator does not need a videotape to see what she or he looks like to students sitting in the rows of desks. One can simply turn on a "news" channel and listen to the never-ending drone of the "talking heads" rambling on and on about their "expert" views. After a few painful viewings, the old-style teacher may develop a healthy level of empathy for the students who are forced to listen to the classroom lectures. A shift in teaching style may occur and have been more effectively stimulated by a TV news panel than by attendance at any over-priced conference; *see also, Canned Presentations, Conferences, Journalism, Unit of Study.*

**TAXPAYERS** In an interesting choice of word usage, public sector bureaucrats and politicians rarely use the term citizens to describe the population. People are referred to as "taxpayers" as if their main purpose was to act as a fountain of finance for the government and its operations, public schools included.

**TEACHER OF THE GIFTED** Why is it that more than a few teachers assigned to teach gifted students seem to think that they must share the same intellectual ability as their charges? These teachers, self-described gifted people that they are, are often proficient at edubabble to further demonstrate their high intellectual ability; *see also, G and T, One Hundred Thirty-Two, Quibble (3).*

**TEACHER SHORTAGE – MATH AND SCIENCE** Teachers with certain academic credentials may find it difficult to parlay their background into more lucrative occupations outside of education. Not so with those teachers holding Math and Science degrees, particularly if their academic background is strong. Gainful employment can be found in an exciting range of occupations in the world of science and technology, with salary and advancement opportunity far surpassing that available in teaching.

With occupational opportunities outside education and the popularity of STEM (Science, Technology, Engineering, and Math) within the school system, a shortage of Math and Science teachers is possible, if not probable. There may come a time when these teachers will need to be incentivized to a greater degree than their colleagues. This will make an interesting dilemma shared by school district employers and teacher unions as the equal-compensation-for-all principle may be challenged; *see also, Chemistry Teachers.*

**TEACHERS' ASSOCIATION** This is the preferred term as it sounds much more refined than labor union.

**TERM-DROPPER** Using fifty-dollar words when dime ones will do is only effective when the person at the other end of the conversation is lacking the sufficient vocabulary to respond in kind or up the ante. A person must be careful about firing off edubabble to everyone. Eventually a more skilled term-dropper will be encountered. If a person never understood what the fifty-dollar term being used really meant, trouble is on the horizon when a hundred-dollar one is flung back. For maximum effectiveness, edubabble should be used with non-teacher parents, or politicians holding a high school level of education or less; *see also, Edubabble-Characteristics, Name-Dropper, Questions in Interviews-Strategy One.*

**TEXTBOOK** It is not surprising that some students logically believe this old-style learning resource to a combination of texting and Facebook; *see also, Mishaps of Classroom Technology, Screen Addicts, Thumb Tapping.*

**THEFT** Security systems in schools are usually less than state-of-the-art. The few measures that do exist are directed toward student miscreants. Formal equipment inventories are rarely done and there is often a blurred line between those books and materials that are the teacher's property and that which belongs to the school.

Teachers are an astonishingly honest bunch. Given the computers, sports paraphernalia, robotics equipment, shop tools, and software programs, very little is stolen. If teachers are to engage in theft, it is more likely to be without malice and confined to scads of pens and pencils and a few pads of writing paper, all of which are dirt cheap and of marginal utility in the hi-tech era.

**THINKING** When thinking about thinking, is it better to start with Convergent or Divergent forms? And why would someone think about that? *see also, Lateral Thinking, Meta-Cognition, Quibble (4).*

**THUMB TAPPING** Just as keyboarding became a "must-be-taught" skill in the 1980s and 90s, efficient thumb-tapping may indicate a school's commitment to provide students with relevant curriculum and twenty-first-century skill development; *see also, First Day Fashion, Knitting, Screen Addicts, Textbook, XYZ.*

**TIME VAMPIRES** A teacher will likely encounter a mother bear at some point in time—a beast which hovers, helicopter-like over her teenage son or daughter. She takes oodles of teacher time, before school, after school, at night, and on the weekend through incessant texting. She sucks up more time than Dracula drank blood. Encountering one of these parents may lead the teacher to search for a Christian cross and a wooden stake; *see also, Negative Nobility, Work-Life Balance.*

**TOP DESK DRAWER** The contents of the front section of the top drawer of a teacher's desk are well known. Everyone pulls out the drawer just far enough to locate and snatch oft-used items. The back area is another matter since the drawer is rarely pulled out past halfway. At the end of the school year a teacher might attempt to clear out the entire drawer. When that occurs, some interesting items may be found, such as:

a) half-melted breath-mints, covered in dust and grime;

b) a dozen pens, none of which work;

c) contraband confiscated from students, months previously;

d) tickets for a special promotion run by a local business that were not distributed;

e) scraps of paper with telephone numbers scrawled in pen or pencil;

f) felt pens and markers, now dry.

**TOXICITY PIT** When there are upward of one hundred teachers in a large high school, the odds are that there will be a cadre of toxic colleagues. Fortunately, in most schools their numbers are usually small. But what these people lack in body-count they can make up for in verbosity. Since toxicity can spread like a virus, it is best to make specific seating arrangements in the teachers' lounge so that these colleagues can get to know each other better. There they can "sing to the choir" and whine to like-minded colleagues about whatever issue is at the forefront that day or week. The majority of the teachers can then engage in pleasant conversation in another section of the room; *see also, Deadline, Kleenex Box, Meeting Behavior-Teachers (e), White Noise (a).*

**TRANSFER** At times teachers remain in an assignment a bit too long and perspective begins to narrow. Some hints that it may be time to consider a transfer are when you:

a) begin to complain about student behavior and motivation in your honors-level senior Physics class;

b) insist that the top students in your Developmental Special Education class are as academically able as those in regular classes;

c) teach the grandchildren of former students the same grade level or subject.

**TUBA** *see Euphonium.*

# U

**UNDER THE BUS** If there has been a decline in test scores, a rise in teen pregnancy rates, an increase in political extremism among youth, or a spike in obesity, there is a good chance that at least a few politicians will throw the public-school system and the teachers who work in it under the bus. The presence of handy scapegoats makes explanation easy; *see also, Drop Out Rate, Ethical Standards, Juul.*

**UNFRIEND** In yet another gadget-driven butchering of the English language, this tech-originating term refers to removing someone from your Facebook link. Following the logic, if a teacher removes a pupil from class is that action an example of "unstudent"; *see also, David and Goliath (6).*

**UNIFORMS - STUDENT** Clothing is remarkably similar from student to student and is a kind of uniform of individuality. The formal uniform issue is occasionally promoted by the extreme political right and left displaying rare agreement. Many of the conservative-right believe that student uniforms help bring a level of decorum to the school. The socialist-left believe that uniforms can help remove the "stain of affluence" from student attire.

Like many political issues, talk is cheap, and where it has been implemented, the supposed benefits of uniforms do not often match the positives so extolled; *see also, Boarding School Syndrome.*

## UNINTERRUPTED SUSTAINED SILENT READING

The acronym for this practice, USSR, was not politically correct in the Reagan era, perhaps stimulating the DEAR label that is now more popular (Drop Everything and Read). Given that the USSR no longer exists, is may be assumed that the United States "won" the Cold War. Even though Russia is only one part of the former USSR, it was the largest and most powerful of the republics. With Russian interference in American elections seemingly accepted by at least some US politicians, perhaps the USSR moniker is now best described as Uninterrupted Sustained Scheming Retribution.

## UNIQUENESS OF SCIENCE TEACHERS

1. Climate change, electric vehicles, habitat reduction, ocean pollution, nuclear energy; these topics are among many contemporary issues that have captured considerable media attention. Unfortunately, emotion and politics can trump

science and muddy these waters. Everyone has an opinion about these topics, though very few have any real scientific knowledge to support their often-doctrinaire views. Science teachers are unique, not that they lack opinions on these matters, but they actually know something about the science involved.

2. Scientists have an image of being somewhat "different." A multitude of B-level movies featuring the "crazed" Dr. Frankenstein helped establish the image. It was burnished by characters such as Christopher Lloyd's offbeat Doc Brown in the *Back to the Future* movies and Mr. Spock in the *Star Trek* franchise. Photos of the unruly-haired Albert Einstein added to the mystique. But it not just these apparent traits that make science teachers and scientists unique. In the United States they are one of the few who are conversant with the metric system. Being able to switch from yards to meters, miles to kilometers, and pounds to kilograms makes it seem as if they can speak a foreign language; *see also, Chemistry Teachers, Kilometer, Miles and Inches.*

**UNIT OF STUDY** Before the era of self-directed, student-centered learning, this was a teacher-generated grouping of content. The unit concluded with a formal evaluation activity, usually a test. Since teacher-direction, facts and content, and formal evaluation appear to moving out-of-favor with the education theorists, it is best that teachers using content-heavy, unit-ending tests undertake such activity in as clandestine manner as possible; *see also, Optical Mark Reader.*

**UNIVERSITY ADMISSION** The criteria for admission are listed in the university calendar. Despite the appearance of an immovable series of entrance standards, there is always a little "wiggle room" in response to some "massage oil" that can grease the wheels of decision-making. In these cases, substitute a cash endowment in place of massage oil.

While such practice may occur on occasion in status-driven private high schools, there are very few nefarious public-school bureaucrats willing to dip their toe into these roiling waters. Firstly, greasing the wheels for admission is a waste of time when everyone is welcomed. Secondly, the only activity with potential for a little kickback influence is limited to final grades in senior courses leading to university admission. Finally, and most importantly, this is an ethical line that extremely few people in public education are willing to cross; *see also, Ethical Standards, Robotics Competitions.*

**UNSCHOOLERS** There are the alternate schoolers who wish to attend a non-traditional school. There are the homeschoolers, many of whom have some connection to the public system through computer-generated distance or distributed education. Then there are the unschoolers who do not want a connection with any education authority. Eventually, several of these unschoolers attend school in their teens when the student is of an age to exert some influence over his or her education.

Sometimes the student is at grade level in reading and writing. Most often, the newly enrolled unschooler lags far behind in Mathematics and Science. In some cases, the adolescent unschooler has received very little instruction at all, being allowed to wander the streets or having been coerced into working in the family home-based business. With academic skills lagging far behind peers, the school's teachers are expected to work miracles and jump-start the unschooler's skills to make up for what can be a decades-long gap in two or three years. Jumper cables are useful for sparking car engines but they don't do much for a quick boost in basic academic skills.

Good luck! *see also, Norms.*

**UPHILL BOTH WAYS** When a person spends a career working with young people it is natural to become frustrated from time to time, especially when teaching those inhabiting the middle class and above in the socioeconomic strata. At times it may seem as if these students are spoiled and indulged to a point of entitlement beyond anything the teacher remembers as a youth. The urge to explain how tough it was in the olden days can become difficult to resist. If the urge strikes to regale the teen it is best to avoid hyperbole. Stick to truthful time-honored gems such as, "We didn't have the internet to help with the research," or, "We didn't have TVs in our bedrooms, there was only one in the house, and it only had twenty channels!"

Unfortunately, it is easy to get carried away and engage in a little exaggeration, "We had to walk seven miles to school each day and it was uphill both ways!" is a statement that defies science. Even in an era of fake news the comment is not likely to deceive a savvy contemporary teen; *see also, Millennial Teachers.*

# V

**VACATION SERVANT** Mom and dad have decided to take the family to Mexico in the middle of February for two weeks. The adults will devour inexpensive food and beer. The kids will be boogie-boarding and lolling around on the beach. The parents expect the teacher to concoct a series of projects for the students so they can keep up with their schoolwork. There is only a miniscule chance any of the work will be done.

When the students return home, smiling and tanned, the parents will expect the teacher to develop another set of work since the class has "moved on" while they were on vacation. Time will be required for the students to complete the new work. The teens will need to "catch-up" and it is the teacher's responsibility to assist with extra tutoring. Is it any wonder that the teacher feels as much of a servant as those who brought the parents the beer on that distant sunny beach?

**VALLEY VIEW** Along with Mountain View, this must be one of the most common names for schools that are not named after a President. Why are school boards so interested in tacking "View" onto the name of a school? After all, students and teachers are indoors most of the day and gazing starry-eyed out the window is not normally encouraged.

**VALUE OF EDUCATION** For a moment let's park most teachers' views of the value of education, such as personal growth, self-actualization, balanced life, joy of learning etc., and focus on what really matters to many people; money. The United States Bureau of Labor churns out reams of statistics, one of them being the monetary value of specific levels of education. In April 2018 they published weekly earnings figures from the year previously according to education level attained. Those with less than a high school education earned around $500.00 per week. Those with Bachelor's degrees earned more than double that, coming in at around $1,150 per week. People holding professional degrees made the most money, slightly more than those with doctorates, at $1,850.00 weekly.

**VANGUARD** The desire to be vanguard—cutting edge, leading edge, razor edge, canyon edge, or any other edge, does not last long in teaching, probably two to three failed innovations at most. The edges are too hard, it's a long way to fall, and the people talking you into taking the plunge usually don't know anything about teaching.

**VAPING** *see Juul.*

**VARNEY THE VAMPIRE** Published as a serialized story, this "penny dreadful" fiction between 1845 and 1847 pre-dated Bram Stoker's *Dracula* by fifty years. It introduced many of the traits commonly associated with vampires including the fangs that leave two puncture marks on the neck, the hypnotic powers, and the vampire's habit of sweeping in through the always-open window to have its way with an unsuspecting maiden. These gothic horror stories continue to be favored by young adults. They are enjoying a notable spike in popularity in the twenty-first century and the possible reasons for such may best be left to the psychologists and sociologists.

A teacher may want to assign *Varney* as an introduction to the gothic horror genre. This is not a good idea. The author was paid by the typeset line, so there are 232 chapters and 667,000 (not a typo) words (most novels are in the 100,000-word range); *see also, Young Adult Gothic Horror.*

**V-BUCKS** This is the currency that is used in the "free" video game, Fortnite, which has taken youth by storm in the 2017-20 period. A teacher may wonder why a currency is required in a "free" game. If a teacher has not heard of Fortnite, he or she may wish to read the two specific entries describing the game's impact; *see also, Fortnite, World Cup of Fortnite.*

**VENDING MACHINES** The presence of these contraptions in schools is under considerable pressure from the culinary correctness crowd. Despite this, many machines still remain. They are stocked with what most describe as "junk food" since kale, quinoa, and such are unlikely to be popular choices from a vending machine. If a school still has these mechanical junk-food dispensaries, students can always grab a bag of cheezies or a chocolate bar on their way to their Foods and Nutrition class; *see also, Culinary Correctness, David and Goliath (3), Kale, Quinoa.*

**VIRTUAL FIELD TRIP** With the growing popularity of virtual reality, it may not be long before field trips are "old news." Why take the time to cajole the principal into releasing the funds, distribute and collect permission slips, and order a bus when the students can strap on a headset and travel virtual-reality style to the local museum? As the technology becomes more refined and destinations more available, perhaps a virtual trip to the Louvre in Paris or the British Museum in London is in order? An added bonus is that the virtual reality field trip to Europe does not include the teacher having to worry about the students quaffing French wine or warm English beer.

**VISUAL LEARNING** Some good edubabblers use this catch-all phrase to include teaching methodologies such as Graphic Organizing and Webbing. The term Visual Learning not only sounds impressive, it connects well with the trend to attach any adjective to the word learning; *see also, Edubabble-Characteristics (e), Experiential Learning, Situated Learning.*

**VIXEN** There is legitimate cause for concern if this term is used by other adults to describe a female teacher's persona and behavior while at work. Other descriptors such as sultry and vamp are similarly undesirable; *see also, Studmuffin.*

**VOCATIONAL DREAMS** By definition dreams are not reality nor likely to become so. Examples of youthful vocational dreams that may require a rethink at some point in time are:

a) the senior-age basketball player who has biological parents under 5 feet 7 inches tall who wishes to be an NBA or WNBA star;

b) the teen who is achieving 22% in Science class who wishes to be an astrophysicist;

c) the music student who is struggling to chord-thump between 'G' and 'C' on the guitar who longs to be a rock star.

# W

**WATER FOUNTAINS** Why would students use water fountains when they or their parents can purchase water contained in plastic bottles which eventually make their way into the local landfill, a river, or the ocean?

**WEAPONS OF MASS DISTORTION** Words have always been an effective weapon as the old adage, "The Pen is Mightier Than the Sword" attests. In today's world, the deluge of information from a plethora of sources makes it difficult for teachers to assist students in drawing the distinction between truth and fiction. The line between the intent to inform and the desire to distort has become blurry at best. A less well-known phrase is becoming more dominant, "If you say something often enough to enough people, it will eventually become the truth."

The only defense against such distortion is a well-educated citizenry. This demands a vibrant public-school system as the logical vehicle to use in combatting the trend; *see also, Anti-Educators (a), Congress,*

*Digital Citizenship, Ethical Standards, Fiction and Reality, Journalism.*

**WEBSITE PROJECT** Assigning a task to develop a website is a sound educational project for a Graphic Design or Computer Technology course. A little tinkering can add a touch of Art History and make the project really interesting. Have students investigate a famous artist and then imagine and design a website that the artist would have likely fashioned.

The students will have many artists to choose from as well as a variety of eras and styles. The student(s) who choose Salvador Dali will have made one of the most intriguing choices. His unusually long, thin mustache, flamboyant personality, eccentric manner, and knack for self-promotion would be fascinating to many high school students. His prolific career, dominated by surreal images, adds much to the mystique.

What a project — attempting to answer the question, "If Salvador Dali were alive today, what would his website look like?" *see also, Expulsion from School (1), Hotbeds of Dissent, New Art Form.*

**WEED** If a principal is tiring of the rambunctious critics at teacher meetings, a little weed slipped into the bran muffins (only where it is legal of course) might make for a more docile gathering with enjoyably compliant teachers; *see also, Bake Sale Comeback, Culinary Correctness, Gateway Drug, Meeting Behavior–Teachers (b), Quarterback (b), Zoned Out.*

**WHAT WERE THEY THINKING?** You have to be a veteran or retired teacher to remember the common practices in schools that, by today's standards, border on lunacy:

a) Smoke-filled air that choked those sitting in the teachers' lounge; *see also, Love That Nicotine;*

b) The PE teachers telling a few of the top athletes in the class to pick their teams from classmates who were lined up along a gymnasium wall—the same student always being chosen last and being ridiculed for it; *see also, In the Gym, Yoga;*

c) Boys who were sent home for having hair that was too long (1969) and then too skinhead-short ten years later;

d) The retention of struggling students for an entire year rather than provide access to specialized services; *see also, Special Education;*

e) Miscreant students receiving corporal punishment by being strapped by a belt-wielding principal.

With hindsight, sometimes the "good old days" were not always so good.

**WHITE NOISE** When a teacher hears the same sound over and over, it soon becomes white noise. Some examples in schools include:

a) the yapper colleagues who dominate the teachers' lounge with the same spiel every day; *see also, Know-It-All Colleague, Toxicity Pit;*

b) the principal who launches into a lengthy monologue at every staff meeting; *see also, Monologue;*

c) the hum of the fluorescent lights in the classroom or hallway;

d) the profanity heard in the high school hallway and grounds; *see also, F-Bomb, Obscenity and Profanity.*

**WOMEN'S SUFFRAGE** An initial glance at this entry may lead one to believe it is focused on women suffering through the stories of self-aggrandizing male colleagues, or struggling to meet the demands of balancing teaching with household chores. Despite the seemingly obvious link to pain and suffering, this term means women achieving the right to the vote.

Teachers have been on the forefront of social change in the current era and in the past. An example of this latter point is the National Education Association (NEA) supporting women's suffrage in 1912, eight years before it happened nationally in the United States; *see also, Genderqueer.*

**WORK-LIFE BALANCE** Not even billionaire professional athletes or big business CEOs are expected to work twenty-four hours a day, seven days a week. But that is what some parents believe their teen's teacher should be doing. The teacher receives emails about homework, field trips, assignment grading, upcoming classroom activities, bullying, and much more. These pile into the inbox any time of the day or night. Of course, the teacher is expected to provide a response to whatever cyberspace missive has been launched within a reasonable amount of time, reasonable being regarded as ten minutes. Given this deluge of requests, complaints, and comments, it is becoming more and more difficult for the teacher to achieve some kind of work-life balance; *see also, Time Vampires.*

**WORKSHOP SELECTION** Though workshops are intended to bolster knowledge, improve skills, or refine perspective, the activity rarely meets with success. If given the choice, teachers, like other adults, tend to choose workshop topics which they already are proficient in or knowledgeable about.

**WORLD CUP OF FORTNITE** This World Cup is not as big as the soccer extravaganza, at least not yet. The 2019 Fortnite gaming competition held in New York boasted one hundred million dollars in prizes, one million each week until the finals. It is intended for thirteen to seventeen-year-olds (with parent permission) who tap away in the hopes of hitting the gaming jackpot. Even high school football teams in Texas cannot come close to this financial largesse.

Teachers should not be alarmed if they are unaware of this competition. They do not have the time to spend ten to twelve hours a day playing Fortnite in a darkened cubby hole of the house or apartment. However, if a teacher is seeking an alternative career path more lucrative than their current occupation, this gaming "work" may be the ticket. The teens currently competing will age and the likelihood of adult-level World

Cups in the future is very likely; *see also, Fortnite, Screen Addicts, V-Bucks.*

**WRESTLING** Those students who dream of dressing in ludicrous costumes and screaming like banshees while leaping off the top rope onto a hapless opponent will likely be disappointed after attending the wrestling team's first practice. In their minds, whoever "invented" the Olympic-style of wrestling used in schools was a "loser," and the sport is typical of the school taking a good thing and making it boring. The WWE wannabes might demand a Mixed Martial Arts team until they realize that the school could even make that bare-knuckled mayhem dull.

**WRITING - CURSIVE** The illegible scrawl of highly paid doctors indicates that even before computers and texting one did not have to be a competent cursive writer to be successful. Now everyone can be just as inept as those in the medical field since the skill is losing whatever importance it once had. Decades ago, good penmanship was an admired craft, at least among traditionalist teachers. Now cursive writing can join other student skills that do not have the cachet they once did, such as:

1. Deciphering a few phrases of Latin.
2. Efficiently moving a slide rule from side-to-side and nodding with confident understanding at the results.
3. Sewing a blouse, skirt, or dress that actually comes

close to fitting the intended person.

4. Reciting the list of presidents from George Washington to the current day.

5. Memorizing a stanza, verse, or an entire poem; *see also, Thumb Tapping.*

# X

**XANAX** If teachers have not yet heard of this medication it is an unfortunate likelihood that they will at some point in their careers. According to the Center for Disease Control and Prevention there is virtually the same number of children ages 3-17 diagnosed with anxiety (4.4 million) as those diagnosed with a behavioral disorder (4.5 million). For those students seeking immediate relief from an anxiety attack (often linked to school attendance), Xanax is the most commonly prescribed medication, more so than Valium and Ativan. Though it is a benzodiazepine ("bennies" in the old street term) with a probability of addiction, the medication is prescribed to children and teens. Like Ritalin, it will likely be more commonly heard in teachers' lounges in the future; *see also, Catastrophizing.*

**X AND Y** Arithmetic deals with basic computation of numbers. Algebra deals with unknown quantities in combination with numbers. In elementary school the child may enjoy proficiency in arithmetic. Then, somewhere in middle school, a teacher will innocently say, "Let's just rub out that '5' from the board and slip in the letter 'x'." The teacher knows that this first occasion will result in some befuddlement from the students, so a gentle, "Just for a minute, okay?" is added. Within two weeks the board will be filled with 'x' and 'y' and then 'a' and 'b'. By high school the student will be hard pressed to find any number not attached to a letter, leaving the student to wonder what the hell happened to all the numbers so fondly recalled from elementary school days?

**XMAS CONCERTS** In many jurisdictions Xmas is now politically and culturally incorrect. However, more than a few parents will be upset at the school shifting away from Christmas traditions. To calm the savage beast of Christian opinion, a performance could include a few pieces such as "Frosty the Snowman", "Silver Bells," or "Rudolf the Red-Nosed Reindeer." Though these songs have nothing to do with the birth of Jesus Christ, their inclusion will likely help pacify the traditionalists.

**XYLOPHONE** This is a good choice of instrument for a relatively uninterested ninth-grade student struggling through a beginner band class. From the student's perspective there is much to like, with some examples being:

    a) The instrument is too cumbersome to be carted home in a car or on the school bus so there is no teacher expectation of daily practice;

b) There may only be a few occasions in an entire musical piece when the instrument comes into play, thus making ongoing errors unlikely (there is the danger of dozing and missing the cue);

c) The instrument requires the use of a small hammer to strike the keys. This puts an attack implement in the student's hands and the obvious opportunity to bong the skull of friend and foe alike; *see also, Knitting.*

**XYZ** If you are a male teacher and you notice that female students in the class are grinning and smirking while texting like demons, you may want to check your tech device. The students may be sending you a message. If it reads 'xyz' you are in the middle of an embarrassing moment which is likely to get a bit worse when an attempt at correction is made. Xyz is tech-abbreviated speech for, "Examine your zipper"; *see also, Thumb Tapping.*

# Y

**YAWNING** Most teachers have a great deal of patience, it being a necessary attribute when working with young people. But one student activity will test the calm demeanor of the most easy-going teacher, a student yawning in exaggerated fashion with hands failing to cover the mouth. The natural teacher reaction is to respond with annoyance. While that may not be the most effective action, it is clearly better than throwing an object or mocking the offending student by respond-ing-in-kind. A yawning contest is one that the teacher cannot possibly win. It will, however, provide the rest of the students with some entertainment as they sit back and enjoy the show; *see also, Manners-Teaching Of.*

**YEAR-END ACTIVITIY** Report cards need to be com-pleted, exams must be marked, retirement functions demand attendance, staff socials require participation, and personal items should be carted home for the summer lest they be misplaced or damaged. It takes a month of the summer vacation for a teacher to decompress from the last week of school.

**YEAR-ROUND SCHOOLS** Tradition is difficult to break. Originally students did not attend school in the summer because they were needed to work on the farm in a largely agrarian North America. The population is now heavily urbanized and many students have never seen a farm, let alone worked on one. If students are needed to work anywhere in the contemporary economy it is in fast-food "restaurants" and those are year-round hubs of activity.

While a number of school districts have moved to a year-round calendar, the vast majority retain the summer-off model supposedly because, "It's always been done that way"; *see also, Early Public Education.*

**YELLOW SCHOOL BUS** It is difficult to throw around impressive words all the time. Good edubabblers should also know snippets of trivia that are connected to education. The color yellow is seen more easily than any other, explaining why school buses and heavy equipment are painted in that color. Black lettering on a specific hue of yellow is the easiest to see in semi-darkness; *see also, Know-It-All Colleague, Red School House.*

**YOGA** Yoga is a physical, spiritual, and mental exercise and is one of the six orthodox schools in the tradition of Hindu philosophy. That religious aspect of yoga is not one to be encouraged in secular public schools.

However, yoga as exercise (Hatha yoga) has much potential in Physical Education departments by offering an activity for students uninterested in basketball, baseball, and the like. In addition, true to the tendency in western culture to commercialize just about everything, there is a plethora of career opportunities surrounding yoga-type exercise; retreats, mats, videos, books and all manner of clothing.

Is there an opportunity for high school yoga class to be part of a unique inter-departmental link between PE, Business, and Career Guidance programs? *see also, In the Gym, Jell-O, What Were They Thinking?* (b), *Xmas Concerts.*

**YOUNG ADULT GOTHIC HORROR** One of the most popular and enduring genres of literature for young adults (roughly those 12-18 years old) is gothic horror. There is something about vampires, demons, decrepit castles, maidens in distress, and copious amounts of blood, that appeals to young adults, especially boys (though the genre is becoming popular with girls as well). Teachers who assign Edgar Allen Poe tales and Bram Stoker's *Dracula* will not likely face controversy. However, it is best for a teacher to pre-read any contemporary gothic-horror stories to determine if the adult stomach can handle the gore. If the pre-read is done at home, ensure that the windows and doors are shut and be prepared for some sleepless nights; *see also, Varney the Vampire.*

# Z

**ZEE TO ZED** A teacher exchange is an excellent way to live in different environs while learning about education in another jurisdiction. Next-door Canada, aside from French-speaking Quebec, presents an opportunity for English-speaking American teachers. Some new English-language spelling will need to be learned. There is no zee in Canada, the final word in the alphabet is pronounced zed. When teaching Art make sure the students are colouring, not coloring. Students should demonstrate good behaviour as opposed to behavior. Keeping with the trend that Canadians like to add letters, a teacher may need to sit in judgement, not judgment, and write cheques not checks.

Aside from the differences in spelling, the teacher can enjoy various forms and flavors of marijuana, consumption of which is legal throughout the country. Any firearms should remain at home, but bring a primer on ice hockey. The exchange teacher should also get used to hearing frequent praises of universal health care.

**ZEROES NOT GIVEN** On occasion there is a point of view put forward in education that is so ludicrous it can qualify as edubabble. Some educators higher up the food chain than teachers have instituted polices forbidding assigning zeroes if student work is not submitted or a test not taken. The essence of their argument was, "How can you grade or punish something that was not there?"

Following that logic into the "real" world, a sports team that does not arrive for a scheduled match should not lose the game by default, or an auditioning actor should not be eliminated from contention just for missing the only casting call.

**ZERO JUDGMENT REQUIRED** Rules that are stead-fast have the appearance of being effective since they are simple. And everyone, well almost everyone, can count. Duplicating the, "Three strikes you're out" from the criminal justice system, some schools have rules such as, "Three truancies equals suspension." Why a few teachers and principals would want to eliminate their professional discretion and decision-making is an interesting question. Perhaps they don't trust their judg-ment or perhaps it is too much of a challenge to use it? Exercising judgment is far more difficult than counting to three.

Eventually this system's weaknesses will be exposed. Using the truancy example above, if a student skipped class on September 11 and again on September 14, then attended school every day until June 2 of the following calendar year before missing one class, does suspending that student according to the "Three strikes and you're out rule" really make sense?

**ZONED OUT** This term used to apply solely to those vacant or sleepy teenagers sitting at the rear of classrooms. Unfortunately, these students still occupy those spots today, but often the source of the behavior is screen, not narcotics, addiction.

These screen-addicted students are totally immersed in their own world of hypnotic visuals flashing across a tiny screen. It takes a great deal of effort for a teacher to break through the student haze. Common strategies such as silence, raising a voice, or even a hand on a shoulder, are rarely effective. Other strategies such as ridiculing the offender, blowing a whistle in his or her ear, or pulling the fire alarm, may be more effective but are clearly not appropriate; *see also, Droning, Fortnite, Gateway Drug, Screen Addicts.*

CPSIA information can be obtained
at www.ICGtesting.com
Printed in the USA
BVHW032037250920
589686BV00001B/9